Exploring Data

An Alternative Unit for Representing and Analyzing One-Variable Data

GLENCOE
Mathematics Replacement Units

GLENCOE

McGraw-Hill

New York, New York
Columbus, Ohio
Mission Hills, California
Peoria, Illinois

Development of the Unit

Exploring Data is one of two units developed under the auspices of the **Making Mathematics Accessible to All Project.** The project is a statewide, cooperative effort among Michigan higher education institutions and intermediate and local districts to assist high schools in reshaping their mathematics programs to provide a common core of broadly useful mathematics for *all* students. The project is supported by a grant from the Dwight D. Eisenhower Mathematics and Science Education Program. In addition to conducting staff development programs for school-based teams consisting of a pair of teachers, a guidance counselor, and an administrator, and conducting follow-up workshops for teachers, the project has also developed a unit titled *Predicting from Data* which is also published by Glencoe.

Send all inquiries to:
Glencoe/McGraw-Hill
936 Eastwind Drive
Westerville, Ohio 43081

ISBN: 0-02-824206-8 (Student Edition)
ISBN: 0-02-824207-6 (Teacher's Annotated Edition)

1 2 3 4 5 6 7 8 9 10 VH/LH-P 03 02 01 00 99 98 97 96 95 94

Table of Contents

Teacher's Handbook

This Teacher's Annotated Edition includes the Student Edition together with Teacher notes and suggested solutions. The unit consists of 5 Investigations which are each made up of Activities. Each activity is designed around the following instructional model which is an adaptation and extension of one used in the Middle Grades Mathematics Project (MGMP). The MGMP is a program developed at Michigan State University to develop mathematics units for instruction in grades 5 through 8. The National Science Foundation funded the program. This model, like the unit, itself, requires new roles for both students and teachers.

Instructional Model

Motivate and Focus
During this first step, the teacher initiates whole-class discussion of the problem situation or question(s) posed at the beginning of each investigation and related activity. This sets the context for the student work to follow. It provides an opportunity to clarify directions for the group activities. The teacher is the director and moderator.

Explore
The next step involves focused problems/questions related to the *Motivate and Focus* situation where investigation leads to gathering data, looking for patterns, and making conjectures. Students work cooperatively in small groups. While groups are working, the teacher circulates from group to group providing guidance and support. This may entail clarifying or asking questions, giving hints, providing encouragement, and drawing group members into the discussion to help groups work more cooperatively. The materials drive the learning, and the teacher is the facilitator.

Share and Summarize
This utilizes whole-class discussion of results found by different small groups. It leads to a whole-class summary of important ideas or to further exploration of a topic if competing perspectives remain. Varying points of view and differing conclusions that can be justified should be encouraged. The teacher is the moderator.

Assess
A group task is used to reinforce initial understanding of the concept or method. The teacher circulates around the room assessing levels of understanding. The teacher is the intellectual coach.
Depending on the goals of the activity, there may be additional *Explore, Share and Summarize, Assess* sequences. An overall class discussion and synthesis by the teacher should occur at the end of each investigation.

Related Applications
This involves a set of related or new contexts to which student-developed ideas and methods can be applied. A subset of these additional applications should be assigned for further group work in class and/or for individual work outside of class. Decisions should be based on student performance and the availability of time and technology. Students should exercise some choice of applications to pursue; at times they should be given opportunity to pose their own problems/questions to investigate. The teacher circulates around the room acting as facilitator and coach.

Extensions
Finally, students work on exercises which permit further or deeper/more formal study of the topic under investigation. Every student should have the opportunity to complete one or more of these extensions during the course of a unit.

Grouping Your Students

This unit has been designed for use in classrooms containing students of diverse backgrounds. In order to ensure heterogeneous grouping, you should make the final decision about group assignments based on mathematical performance levels, gender, and cultural backgrounds at the beginning of each investigation. Students can be re-grouped later in an investigation for related applications and extensions.

If your students have not previously experienced small-group cooperative learning, you will need to present some guidelines for group behavior. These should included:

- Listen carefully and with respect to each other and try, whenever possible, to build on the ideas of each other.
- Make sure everyone contributes to the group task and no one person dominates.
- Ask for clarification or help when something is not understood and help others in the group when asked.
- Achieve a group answer or solution for each task.
- Make sure everyone understands the solution before sharing it with the class or before the group goes on to the next task.

Expect that group work will go more smoothly on some days than others. It usually takes about three weeks for students to begin functioning well in groups. From time to time, remind students of the above guidelines for cooperative group behavior.

More information about cooperative learning can be found in Glencoe's *Cooperative Learning in the Mathematics Classroom*.

Assessing Your Students

Instruction and assessment are closely linked. Both the Student Edition and Teacher's Annotated Edition provide tasks for group as well as individual assessment. The Teacher Suggestions and Strategies also provide suggestions for methods of informal assessment of student performance based on observations. The nature of the Student Edition and the small group format are ideally suited to assessment of mathematical thinking, communication, and disposition toward mathematics through student observations.

For more information on performance assessment, see Glencoe's *Alternative Assessment in the Mathematics Classroom*.

Using Journals and Portfolios

Journals and portfolios are important forms of assessment. Students will find journal prompts and suggestions for what to include in a portfolio in the margins of the activities.

 Journals A journal is a written account that a student keeps to record what she or he has learned. Journal entries are conducive to thinking about why something has been done. They can be used to record and summarize key topics studied, the student's feelings toward mathematics, accomplishments or frustrations in solving a particular problem or topic, or any other notes or comments the student wishes to make. Keeping a mathematical journal can be helpful in students' development of a reflective and introspective point of view. It also encourages students to have a more thoughtful attitude toward written work and should be instrumental in helping students learn more mathematics. Journals are also an excellent way for students to practice and improve their writing skills.

 Portfolios A portfolio is a representative sample of a student's work that is collected over a period of time. The selection of work samples for a portfolio should be done with an eye toward presenting a balanced portrait of a student's achievements. The pieces of work placed in a portfolio should have more significance than other work a student has done. They are chosen as illustrations of a student's best work at a particular point in time. Thus, the range of items selected shows a student's intellectual growth in mathematics over time.

Students may select the products of activities for inclusion. Bear in mind that the actual selection of the items by the students will tell you what pieces of work the students think are significant. In addition, students should reflect upon their selections by explaining why each particular work was chosen.

The following examples illustrate topics that would be appropriate for inclusion in a portfolio.

- a solution to a difficult or nonroutine problem that shows originality of thought
- a written report of an individual project or investigation
- examples of problems or conjectures formulated by the student
- mathematical artwork, charts, or graphs
- a student's contribution to a group report or investigation
- a photo or sketch of physical models or manipulative
- statements on mathematical disposition, such as motivation, curiosity, and self confidence
- a first and final draft of a piece of work that shows student growth

● Student Diversity

In the *Exploring Data* activities, students are asked to interpret data to discuss and support approaches to problems. Students will have to read charts, write reports, defend solutions, and draw conclusions. The students in your class may not have the same level of proficiency required to carry out and produce such high level forms of communication. Reasons of this diversity include lack of proficiency in English, poor knowledge of mathematical terminology, limited exposure to the rules and use of language in mathematical contexts, and lack of background and experience with technical forms of communication.

To foster participation and effective communication by *all* students, we must try to obtain an idea of the students' communication skills. This can be accomplished by using the students' responses to each investigation opener. Listen to the students as they talk about and interpret the task. Who is having difficulties understanding the requirements? Which students cannot identify and explain the components and objectives of the activity?

Second, examine the written work. Which students cannot fully explain the solution? Is this due to a lack of mathematical knowledge or the inability to express thoughts in written or oral form?

Lastly, you may wish to use the following general strategies to address communication diversity issues.

- Spend the initial phase of the activities clarifying terms, expressions, task requirements, and symbols. Encourage students to offer their interpretations of the problems or task components.

- Encourage students to describe ideas and processes orally in their cooperative learning groups. Many communication skills are developed through practice.

- Let students use their first language in small groups if they are unable to fully communicate mathematical ideas in English.

● Key to Icons in Margin Column

FYI	**FYIs** are "fast facts," entertaining tidbits, and fascinating math-related trivia.
Graphing Calculator Activity	*Exploring Data* contains 5 **Graphing Calculator Activities** that allow students to explore mathematical concepts.
Share and Summarize	These headings suggest class discussion about the results found by different groups.
Portfolio Assessment	A **Portfolio Assessment** suggestion asks students to select items from their work that represent their knowledge.
Journal	A **Journal Entry** appears in many of the activities, giving students the opportunity to keep a written log of their thoughts.

Exploring Data

Unit Overview

● **Why This Unit is Important**

The overall purpose of this unit is to bring students of all abilities in contact with important mathematical ideas and techniques. *Exploring Data* emphasizes representation and analysis of one-variable data. This unit introduces students to a view of mathematics as a science and language of patterns. Graphical representations and visual reasoning plays a fundamental role throughout *Exploring Data*. The unit closes with an investigation of the effects of data transformations on the standard deviation.

● **Investigation Profile**

Investigation 1 Students explore patterns that arise in geometric contexts. Identification and extension of patterns leads to ways of describing and generalizing patterns through the use of tables, verbal rules, symbolic expressions, and graphs. These representation forms and their connections are stressed throughout the unit.

Investigation 2 This investigation fosters cooperative group behavior in the context of collecting and informally analyzing and making inferences from data involving human characteristics. Efforts to make sense of the data lead to issues of typical values or centers, variation, correlation between pairs of variables, and prediction; all of which are explored in subsequent investigations.

Investigation 3 Line graphs, stem-and-leaf plots, and histograms are explored as useful first-steps to examining data. Line graphs enable students to analyze and compare trends in data over time. Their analysis also provides a fertile context for planting the seeds for the graphical analysis of the behavior of functions. Stem-and-leaf plots and histograms are used to help make sense of nutritional data for fast foods and other data in the world of students. A fundamental lesson students learn is that an informative graph and its analysis in terms of center, overall pattern, and deviations always precedes numerical calculations.

Investigation 4 This investigation guides students to descriptive statistics – range, median, mean, mode – for summarizing data as a supplement to graphical displays. These statistics enable students to come to a further understanding of the fast foods data as well as other sets of data . The relationship between the shape of a distribution and the relative location of the mean and the median provides a visual interpretation of the robustness of the median as a measure of center. The effects of data transformations on these statistics are investigated numerically and geometrically. Pattern analysis leads to discovery of properties and their algebraic representations.

Investigation 5 Box-and-whisker plots are explored as a display method that captures the variation in a set of data and also facilitates comparison of multiple sets of data . Mean deviation and standard deviation are investigated for their usefulness in quantifying the amount of variation. With these additional tools, students are able to complete their analysis of the single-variable sets of data examined throughout the unit.

Unit Outcomes

There are three fundamental outcomes of the work in *Exploring Data*.

- Students will be able to recognize and use patterns as a method of understanding their world, including mathematics.

- Students will be able to make sense out of single-variable data by collecting and organizing data and using graphical displays and numerical summaries for analysis and interpretation. They will be able to express and justify their interpretations orally and in writing.

- Students will appreciate the usefulness of graphical, tabular, and numerical-summary representations in making sense of real-world data.

Using Manipulatives and Materials

Cooperative learning activities, which often include the use of manipulatives are the basis for all learning in *Exploring Data*. Below is a list of the manipulatives and materials suggested for this unit. A list specific to each activity also appears at the beginning of the activity.

Manipulative	Activity	Manipulative	Activity
Calculator	1-1, 1-2, 1-3, 4-1, 4-2, 5-1, 5-2	Newspapers/Magazines	3-3
Colored Pencils	3-1	Pattern Blocks	1-2
Centimeter Cubes	1-3	Rulers	3-3, 4-1, 4-2, 5-1
Flat Toothpicks	1-1	Scissors	2-1
Graph Paper	3-1	Software	3-3, 4-1, 5-1, 5-2
Map of the United States	5-1	Tape Measure	2-1
		Tracing Paper	1-2, 5-1

Using *Exploring Data* with
Merrill Pre-Algebra: A Transition to Algebra
Merrill Algebra 1: Applications and Connections,
Merrill Geometry: Applications and Connections, and
Merrill Algebra 2 With Trigonometry: Applications and Connections

Exploring Data consists of five Investigations that may be used as alternative or supplemental materials for *Merrill Pre-Algebra, Merrill Algebra 1, Merrill Geometry* and *Merrill Algebra 2*. The following correlation shows you which Investigation can be used with lessons in each text.

Exploring Data Investigation Number	Merrill Pre-Algebra Lesson Number	Merrill Algebra 1 Lesson Number	Merrill Geometry Lesson Number	Merrill Algebra 2 Lesson Number
1	5-8, 5-9	1-1, 1-7, 6-1, 9-2	6-2, 12-4	2-3, 13-1, 13-2
2	9-9, 10-1,	4-5	13-9	8-2
3	10-1, 10-3, 10-9	9-8, 14-2	9-8	14-1, 14-2, 14-7
4	10-2	14-1, 14-3		14-2, 14-3
5	10-4, 10-5	14-4, 14-5		14-4, 14-5, 14-6

Teaching Suggestions and Strategies

Patterns

Mathematics Overview

This investigation focuses on mathematics as a science of patterns. The concept of variable as a pattern generalizer is introduced informally as students explore patterns of shapes in a plane and in space using manipulatives. Students extend observed patterns and describe patterns of growth first in words and then using variables. The use of, and connections among, tables, graphs, and symbolic representations to express relationships is explored.

Investigation Outcomes

Students will

- extend geometric and numerical patterns;
- describe patterns orally, in writing, and using variables;
- complete a data table;
- transfer data from tabular to graphical representation;
- use patterns to solve problems.

Materials Needed

 *flat toothpicks*

 calculators

 tracing paper

 centimeter cubes

 pattern blocks

Activity 1-1 Representing Patterns

1 Motivate and Focus

Draw students' attention to possible patterns within the classroom: ceiling or floor tiles, arrangement of desks, clothing they are wearing.

Ask a student to hand clap or tap on the desk a favorite song; check if their classmates can recognize it from the pattern of the melody.

Ask a student to describe the pattern of the changing seasons.

2 Share and Summarize

Bring students together after Exercise 7 to discuss their findings and pattern descriptions. Summarize again after Exercises 9 and 11. The extensions, except possibly Exercise 13, are within reach of all students.

3 Extend the Activity

Students could be asked to design a growing pattern from a polygon of their choice and investigate possible relationships. Provide opportunities for students to share their discoveries during the course of the unit.

Students might also be encouraged to write a short paragraph on patterns in another school subject of their choice.

4 Assess the Activity

Observe performance of students as they work in groups. Skill at recognizing and representing patterns develops over time. Avoid formally assessing this skill prematurely

If students are maintaining a journal, ask them to include entries about:

- What was easy about this activity?
- What was difficult?
- Did your group work cooperatively together?
- Why or why not?

Activity 1-2   Using Patterns

1 Motivate and Focus

Show some regular tiling patterns. Ask students to describe them so that types of polygons can be reviewed.

Elicit the idea of a regular polygon through discussion or by using a collection of examples and counterexamples and asking students to determine identifying characteristics of the regular polygons.

The sum of the angle measures of a triangle can be visually seen by having students tear off two of the angles, rearrange them about the vertex of the third angle, and notice that sides form a line or 180°.

2 Share and Summarize

Make sure that students have the correct information in the table of Exercise 4a either by summarizing as a class or by circulating to check the work of each group. Continue on with Exercises 4-8, then return for sharing and closure. Exercise 10 may be used as a homework assignment with students sharing their results later in the week.

3 Extend the Activity

Some of M.C. Escher's art work could be investigated either in class or as an outside-of-class project. As a follow-up to Exercise 9, some students might be encouraged to investigate the number of different tessellations that can be formed using a combination of two or more regular polygons. There are many books available on tessellations.

4 Assess the Activity	Ask students whether a regular polygon having 20 sides could be used repeatedly to tile a showroom floor and to explain their reasoning.

Ask students to describe the conditions where a regular polygon forms a tiling in terms of the number of sides of the polygon.

Activity 1-3 Generalizing Patterns

1 Motivate and Focus

Ask students to describe a cube. This could be done in pairs, as a free-flow writing activity, or as a whole-class discussion. Elicit and discuss the terms: corners, edges, faces, sides, interior, and exterior. Have students build some cubes using centimeter cubes. Ask, "Can you create a large cube out of 50 small cubes?"

2 Share and Summarize

Make sure the data recorded in the table for Exercise 1 is correct. After Exercise 3, summarize with a class discussion. Emphasize visual reasoning as prompted by Exercise 2. Share and summarize after Exercise 4.

Ask students to verbalize the thinking that they used when making the algebraic generalizations. Discuss Exercises 7-10, emphasizing the reasoning. Have some of the groups present their summary for Exercise 11e.

3 Extend the Activity

Students could explore the graphs (Exercise 11) representing their data by using a graphing utility. Other extension ideas are available in the book *Exploring with Squares and Cubes*, Dale Seymour Publishing.

4 Assess the Investigation

Refer students to the growing staircase in Exercise 15 of and ask them to:

a. Draw the fifth shape in the pattern and determine its area and perimeter.

b. Determine the area and perimeter of the 12th shape in the pattern and explain their reasoning.

c. Describe in words how the staircase pattern grows; how the area of the pattern grows; how the perimeter of the pattern grows.

d. Represent the area of a staircase that has n steps.

e. Represent the perimeter of a staircase that has n steps.

Ask students to write a paragraph describing what they learned in this investigation and how it might be useful outside this class.

Collecting Data

The main purpose of this investigation is to give students a firsthand and personal look at data collection and interpretation. This data will be revisited throughout the unit as students develop more formal methods of data analysis. A secondary goal of the investigation is to further acclimate students to working cooperatively in small groups.

● Mathematical Overview

● Investigation Outcomes

Students will

- practice and evaluate various cooperative group behaviors;
- collect and record in tables, data on human characteristics;
- examine human characteristics data and informally explore questions of representativeness and variation and possible relationships between pairs of variables.

● Materials Needed

 tape measures

 scissors

Activity 2-1   Getting to Know Yourself and Others

1 Motivate and Focus

Ask students how data on family size might be used to plan housing developments. Then ask them how this kind of data could be obtained. Inquire as to possible reasons why there appears to be a greater marketing of products for senior citizens today. How is this related to data? Then ask students the following questions.

- How many students in the class wear a size medium T-shirt?
- Are each of these students the same size?
- How are clothing sizes related to data?

2 Share and Summarize

Following the pooling of group data toward the end of each project, conduct a whole class discussion of the remaining questions.

Note that as students progress through this unit they will develop systematic methods that will help them to answer the questions more completely.

3 Extend the Activity

Exercise 4f could be pursued further by collecting data from the rest of the student body and publishing the results in the student newspaper. There will be many additional opportunities for data collection and analysis as students progress through the unit.

4 Assess the Activity

Use Exercise 7 as a group assessment. As an alternative or additional group assessment, have each group identify a question of interest to them, collect appropriate data, and analyze the data to arrive at a possible answer. Then have each student write a short report describing methods and findings.

Displaying Data

● Mathematical Overview

This investigation examines three ways of displaying data–line graphs, stem-and-leaf plots, and histograms. Students read and interpret data from charts, tables, and graphs and produce graphical displays by hand and with technology. In selection of a graphical display for a given set of data, it is expected that students will explain the appropriateness of their choice in terms of its intended use.

The investigation begins with an analysis of line graphs. This analysis assumes prior knowledge of the concept of variable as a quantity that varies (in this case over time). Many of the questions foreshadow basic ideas in the graphical interpretation of functions. The emphasis of the remaining activities is on stem-and-leaf plots or histograms to understand features of sets of data in terms of the shape of the distributions.

● Investigation Outcomes

Students will

- read and interpret data summarized in charts, tables, and graphs;
- produce line graphs, stem-and-leaf plots, and histograms for sets of data;
- select a graphical display for a given set of data and explain its appropriateness in terms of its intended use;
- describe the shape of a distribution in terms of center, symmetry, stretch, clustering and gaps.

● Materials Needed

 graph paper

 colored pens or pencils

 rulers

 newspapers and magazines

 statistical software

Activity 3-1   Line Graphs

1 Motivate and Focus

Ask students which TV program they watched last evening at 8:00 or 9:00. Determine which program had the greater portion of viewers in the class at each time. Connect this survey and results to the Neilson ratings and their uses. Compare student data to Neilson ratings for the previous week. These can be found in *USA Today*, Wednesday edition.

2 Share and Summarize

Whole-class discussion should be held after groups have completed Exercise 9 and again after Exercise 14. Discuss student opinions on the appropriateness of using a graph or a table in the context of answering Exercise 13d or 16e.

**3 Extend
the Activity**

Students could be asked to locate instances of data representations in newspapers or magazines that they think might be more appropriately presented in another form (for example, tables that could have been better represented as graphs or vice versa).

**4 Assess
the Activity**

Observe students as they complete Exercises 12 and 13 and record observations.

Exercise 16 or a line graph from print media with corresponding questions could be used for individual or group assessment .

Activity 3-2   Stem-and-Leaf Plots

**1 Motivate
and Focus**

Food items with labels displaying information about sodium, cholesterol, and calorie content can be brought to class. Discuss why this information is on the labels, what the terms mean, why advertisers use terms such as "low fat," and what "low fat" means.

Discuss the fast foods data given at the beginning of the investigation making sure that students understand the variables and units of measure. Students will access this set of data often in this unit as they develop and apply methods of data analysis.

**2 Share and
Summarize**

After student groups have worked on Exercises 1-8, bring the class together for a whole-class discussion. Use Exercise 4 to highlight the general questions that should always be asked in analyzing the shape of a distribution. Develop a consensus on the method used in Exercise 8.

**3 Extend
the Activity**

Have students collect data on homerun leaders for the National and American League from 1901 to 1994 and use technology to produce a back-to-back stem-and-leaf plot of the data. Then have them write a summary paragraph comparing the performance of the two leagues.

A back-to-back stem-and-leaf plot comparing test or quiz data from two different classes could provide an interesting discussion.

**4 Assess
the Activity**

Exercises 9 and 10 could be used for individual or group assessment.

For group assessment, have each group refer to the class data table they created in Activity 2-1 on page 15 and then prepare and interpret a stem-and-leaf plot for the wrist circumferences.

Individual students could be asked to produce a stem-and-leaf plot for a published table of data of their choice, explain why they chose that particular table, and formulate impressions about the data distribution from the plot.

Have students create a data set that has a particular characteristic such as mounded, triangular, symmetrical with one or two peaks, or stretched to the upper or lower end of the data.

Activity 3-3   Histograms

Students could be asked to bring a graph from a newspaper or magazine or their social studies book to class. Note the frequent use of histograms. Discuss why they are used and how are they produced. To answer the latter question, consider the calorie data.

Note: Using graph paper will contribute to the neatness of student-produced histograms as well as cut down on the time needed to draw them. In most instances, students should use technology to produce histograms.

Have students share their responses following group completion of Exercise 5. Before students begin work on Exercise 6, discuss choosing and displaying the intervals of a histogram. Discuss the following questions.

- Must the interval size always be equal? In this case, the intervals are not equal because of the way they are reported by the Census Bureau.

- How does the display on the horizontal axis differ if the intervals are not equal?

- Be sure that students understand when it is more appropriate to use a stem-and-leaf plot or a histogram and when to use a line graph.

Some of the examples of graphs that may have surfaced during *Motivate and Focus* may include bar graphs and circle graphs. Have students collect examples of bar graphs and describe how they differ from histograms. Have students collect examples of circle graphs and prepare a report describing how they are produced and the kinds of data situations that lend themselves to this kind of representation.

Have students collect and use a histogram to analyze data of their choice or data from a science or social studies class. Data might involve hours of sleep per night by students in a class (grade) or number of years current members of Congress have served in the Senate or House of Representatives.

Have students research the number of graduates of your school who went on to college or to post-secondary training programs over the last 15 years. Analyze the data using the directions given in Exercise 11, parts b-d.

Describing Data

Mathematical Overview

The first activity in this investigation explores measures of center: mean, median, and mode. Students are asked to determine these measures for various sets of data and evaluate the appropriateness of each as a summary statistic. Questions are asked that lead students toward understanding the advantages/disadvantages of each of the mean, median, and mode.

In the second activity, students investigate and make generalizations about transformations of data. The use of graphical displays enable students to "see" the effect of transformations visually as well as numerically. The activity illustrates strong connections among ideas of statistics, geometry, and algebra.

Investigation Outcomes

Students will

- determine the range, mean, median, and mode of a set of data;
- explain how outliers affect measures of center;
- interpret graphically measures of center for a given set of data;
- select a measure of center most appropriate for summarizing a set of data and explain the reason(s) for their choice;
- describe the effects on a set of data and its mean, median, and mode of transforming the data by addition of a constant or multiplication by a constant.

rulers

calculators

Materials Needed

statistical software

Activity 4-1 Measure of Center

1 Motivate and Focus

Ask students how they might describe the typical height of members of their class. Ask "Can this be done without making any measurements? By making at most two measurements?" If a student suggests ordering class members by height and choosing the center person (position), carry out the suggested procedure. Revisit the fast food set of data using this method.

2 Share and Summarize

In Exercise 9, you may wish to point out that in statistics an outlier is officially defined as any value that is more than 1.5 times the interquartile range above the upper quartile or below the lower quartile. However, at this stage students should be encouraged to identify outliers based on an analysis of the shape of the set of data.

Be sure that students understand that the median can only be found using ordered sets of data and that students are calculating it correctly. Whole-class discussion after Exercise 11 should clarify the definition of the mean and mode. Draw from students the idea that a set of data may have no mode, one mode or multiple modes. Exercise 12 requires a major group effort, the results of which should be shared and summarized. Have each student evaluate the foods she or he eats regularly in light of the class conclusions.

Observe groups to be sure that students understand how to compute the median of a set of data with an even number of values and understand that the median does not have to be an actual data entry. Exercises 15-18 may be used as homework. Share and summarize responses to Exercise 17 and note how statistics can be used to misrepresent a situation.

Bring the class together again after Exercise 20 to discuss how the location of the mean and median on a histogram are related to the shape of the graph. Summarize this activity by discussing Exercises 23 and 24.

3 Extend the Activity

Automobile manufacturers are required by law to maintain a fleet minimum for the average fuel consumption on all new models (approximately 24 mpg in 1991). Based on the study of the mean and the way it is influenced by data, have students write a paragraph explaining how auto manufacturers are able to meet the minimum requirements and still continue to build "gas guzzlers."

Have students identify in the news media an instance of use of one of the measures of center and evaluate the appropriateness of the choice of statistic.

4 Assess the Activity

Have students answer Exercise 18 for six numbers and explain how they selected the numbers for their data sets.

Use Exercise 24 as an assessment.

Ask students to describe situations for which each measure of center is the most appropriate.

Give students a computer-generated histogram and ask them to draw the mean and median lines and explain their choice of position.

Ask students to describe a situation when the median will be higher than the mean for a set of data .

Ask "What if McDonald's had a HELP WANTED sign that stated: HELP WANTED: average starting salary over $7? Can this be true? Explain your answer."

Activity 4-2 Patterns in Statistics

1 Motivate and Focus

List a set of test scores and ask students to predict the effect on the mean, median, and mode if points are added to each student's score.

Create a set of data for a basketball player who scores twice as many points in each game the second half of the season as were scored in the first half of the season. Ask students to predict the mean and median points per game for the second half of the season given the mean and median points for the first half of the season.

2 Share and Summarize

This activity should move along quickly. Whole-class discussion of discovered properties should be conducted after Exercise 5 and again after Exercise 11.

3 Extend the Activity

Share the following story with the class.

> Elana calculates her average bowling score for an evening by subtracting 100 from each game score, mentally averaging the new numbers, and then adds 100 back to get her average. Ask students to explain why Elana's method works.

In 1991, the median price of a house in the United States was $99,700. Real estate analysts estimate that housing prices are increasing at 4% per year. Ask students to estimate the median price of a house in the year 2003.

4 Assess the Investigation

Have students toss four coins 20 times and record the number of heads obtained on each toss. Then have them prepare an appropriate graphical display and answer the following questions.

a. What is the median number of heads?

b. What is the mean number of heads?

c. What is the mode of the number of heads?

d. Based on your data, what do you think will be the number of heads most likely to be obtained when four coins are tossed? Explain your reasoning.

More Data Displays

Mathematical Overview

The first activity in this investigation guides students to the development of the five-number summary of a distribution and its graphical representation as a box-and-whisker plot. Box-and-whisker plots are then used as a visual aid to analyze sets of data. Multiple box-and-whisker plots are produced to compare sets of data. Examination of the interquartile range (IQR) displayed in box-and-whisker plots helps students develop an understanding of variation within a data set.

In the second activity, the search for a concept that involves the mean and is parallel to the IQR leads to exploration of the idea of mean variation which in turn leads to the introduction of standard deviation.

The unit closes, as it began, with a study of patterns—in this case, graphical and numerical patterns exhibiting the effect of transformations of data on the standard deviation.

Investigation Outcomes

Students will

- determine the five-number summary: least value, lower quartile, median, upper quartile, and greatest value of a set of data;
- produce and interpret box-and-whisker plots for sets of data;
- use multiple box-and-whisker plots to compare two or more sets of data;
- determine the standard deviation of a set of data;
- use standard deviation to compare the variability of sets of data;
- describe the effect on the standard deviation of a set of data when the data is transformed by addition of a constant or multiplication by a constant.

Materials Needed

 calculator

 tracing paper

 statistical software

 rulers

Activity 5-1 Box-and-Whisker Plots

**1 Motivate
and Focus**

Make an overhead transparency of the data on calories in fast foods on page 24 and the corresponding histogram on page 51. Use these transparencies to solicit from students the method of calculating the median number of calories in the foods and the meaning of this statistic. Lead a discussion regarding the amount of variation in the calorie data. The goal of the activity is to find systematic ways of describing the amount of variation in sets of data.

**2 Share
and Summarize**

After student groups have worked on Exercises 1-4, discuss how the variation is represented in the five-number summary and the box-and-whisker plot. Point out that the median, upper quartile, and lower quartile may not be actual values in the set of data. Whole-class discussion should be conducted after Exercise 9 to discuss the advantages and disadvantages of box-and-whisker plots. Summarize as needed in the remaining exercises.

**3 Extend
the Activity**

Have students prepare a histogram, a box-and-whisker plot, and a stem-and-leaf plot of a set of data of their choice. Then have them write questions pertaining to their data. Pairs of students could then answer each others questions and discuss.

Have students collect data on the calorie or sodium content of meat, all beef, and poultry hot dogs; analyze the data using multiple box-and-whisker plots; and prepare a report summarizing their findings.

**4 Assess
the Activity**

Observe students as they work in groups and evaluate them on their cooperative group efforts.

Ask students to prepare and interpret a box-and-whisker plot from data of their choice.

Ask students to compare two box-and-whisker plots and answer questions regarding them.

Have each group discuss the relative merits of using box-and-whisker plots, histograms, or stem-and-leaf plots with the fast foods data and prepare a report to present to the class.

Activity 5-2 Measures of Variability

1 Motivate and Focus

Have students look at the test scores in Exercise 1. Ask them which test scores are better and why. Alternatively, provide data as points scored by opponents of each of two favorite sports teams (perhaps basketball) and ask which team has the better defense.

2 Share and Summarize

Circulate among the groups, making sure that calculations are correct. Bring students together after Exercise 4 to share results and summarize the meaning of, and the method for, calculating mean deviation. Develop a consensus to Exercise 4c. Groups may delegate the tasks in Exercises 7-9 or you can have each group do a different problem and report on their findings. After Exercise 15, have the students' interests determine the direction of the discussion. At the end of the discussion, students could be asked to predict answers to Exercises 16a and 17a. Students who do the extensions could share their findings.

3 Extend the Activity

Have students choose five whole numbers between 1 and 10 (repeats are allowed) so that the set has the smallest possible standard deviation; the greatest possible standard deviation. Ask, "Is there more than one possible choice for each case? Explain."

4 Assess the Investigation

Exercise 21 in can be used as an individual or group assessment.

Give students the following problem.

> Collect two sets of data (for example, first and second round golf scores, ages of mothers and fathers of students in your social studies class, or prices of normal bias and high bias cassette tapes). Compare them using multiple box-and-whisker plots and appropriate summary statistics. Write a summary paragraph of your findings.

Teacher's Answer Key

Page 4 10.

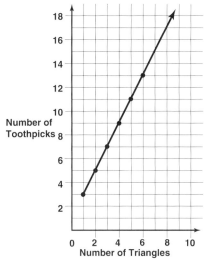

(Graph: y-axis "Number of Toothpicks" 0–18, x-axis "Number of Triangles" 0–10, line passing through plotted points)

Page 5 11b.

13.

Number of toothpicks on one side of the shape	1	2	3	4	5	6
Perimeter in units	3	6	9	12	15	18
Total number of toothpicks	3	9	18	30	45	63

Page 8 4c. First, determine the number of triangles in the polygon (73) and then multiply by 180° to determine the total number of degrees of the polygon. Next, divide the total number of degrees by 75.   **8.** The triangle, square, and hexagon are the only regular polygons that will tile. For a regular polygon to tile, the measures of one angle must be a factor of 360. The factors of 360 are 1, 2, 3, 4, 5, 6, 8, 9, 10, 12, 15, 18, 20, 24, 30, 36, 40, 45, 60, 85, 90, 120, 180, and 360. The factors 60, 90, 120 correspond to a triangle, a square, and a hexagon respectively. There is no regular polygon with angle measure 85 since the number of sides would have to be between 4 and 5. There are no regular polygons with angle measures 180 or 360.

9.

Page 10 2.. The cubes with 3-painted faces are located at each of the top four and bottom four corners of the large cube. The 2-painted faced cubes are on the edges, not including the corner cubes. The 1-painted face cubes are on the sides of the cube, surrounded by the 2- and 3- painted faced cubes. Zero-painted faces are hidden inside the cube; they are the core of the cube.

7.

Number of cubes along an edge	Total number of cubes	Number of cubes with paint on			
		3 faces	2 faces	1 face	0 faces
7	343	8	60	150	125
8	512	8	72	216	216
9	729	8	84	294	343

Page 11 11a.

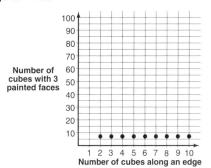

(Graph: y-axis "Number of cubes with 3 painted faces" 0–100, x-axis "Number of cubes along an edge" 1–10, points at 8)

11b.

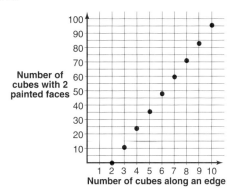

(Graph: y-axis "Number of cubes with 2 painted faces" 0–100, x-axis "Number of cubes along an edge" 1–10)

11c.

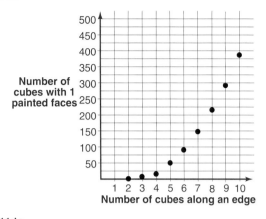

11d.

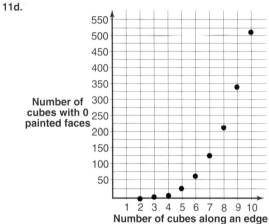

11e. The number of cubes with 3 painted faces stays constant at 8. The number of cubes with 2 painted faces increases along a line. The number of cubes with 1 painted face increases along a curve. The number of cubes with 0 painted faces also increases along a curve, but even faster than the 1 painted face cubes.

Page 14 1e. Sample answer: Class variation should be greater because there are more people.

Page 17 6. One possible method to determine eye dominace: Fold a piece of paper in half and cut out a small semicircle from the center of the paper. Holding the paper at arm's length, sight a distant object through the hole. Without moving your head, close your right eye. If the object disappears, then you are right-eyed dominant.

Page 20 8. Sample answer: Both were down, but college football viewership was down more than college basketball viewership. (Note: This answer requires a comparison of the two graphs.)

Page 22 12b. c. d.

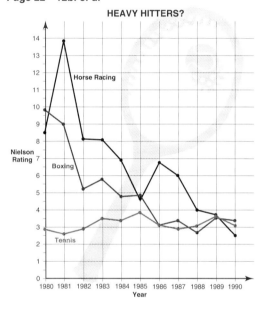

Page 23 16a. The number of milk cows remained fairly constant. The number of beef cows and cattle increased while the number of hogs and pigs decreased. It appears that when there is an increase in cattle there is a decrease in hogs and vice versa.

Page 23 16d.

	1959	**1964**	**1969**	**1974**	**1978**	**1982**	**1987**
Cattle and Calves	92	105	105	116	102	102	98
Hogs and Pigs	68	55	56	45	58	56	52
Beef Cows	25	32	35	41	35	32	30
Milk Cows	16	12	10	9	8	8	8

Page 26 **5**. Sample answers: The stem-and-leaf is better for ordering data from least to greatest, showing clusters and outliers, and locating the center of data. In a stem-and-leaf plot, you lose the name of the food item.

6a.

1	9
2	4 7
3	1 2 2 4 4 4 4 5 7 7 9 9
4	1 1 3 6 9
5	0 0 0 2 3 7
6	1 8
7	
8	
9	3

9|3 = 930

7a.

0	9
1	0 2 2 2 3 3 5 5 5 5 6 8 8 9 9
2	0 0 0 1 4 5 5 6 8 9
3	0 3 6
4	0
5	
6	1

7b. Sample answers: The data appears to have one peak. The center of the data is between 19 and 20. The data stretches to the upper values. There is a gap at the 50's and 61 is an exception.

Page 27 **9b**. Sample answer:

1	
2	7 8
3	0 0 0 1 1 3 4 4 6 7 7 9
4	7
5	2 2 3 3 4
6	0 2
7	
8	0
9	
10	0 0

6|2 = 62,000,000

Page 28 **10c.** Sample answer: The cereals with the most sugar also contain the most calories.

Page 30. **2.** The histogram shows a spread from 100 to 1000 calories. There is a gap between 700 and 900 with only one entry above 900. There is one major peak with the center of the distribution in that interval.

Page 31 **5a.**

Interval	Tally	Frequency
0-9			1
10-19	|||| |||| ||||	14
20-29	|||| ||||	10
30-39	|||	3
40-49			1
50-59		0
60-69			1

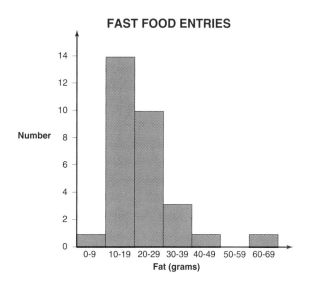

FAST FOOD ENTRIES

6a. See students' histogram. For most intervals, the height is similar but there are two peaks at the 5-19 age and 45-64 age groups. **6b.** See students' histogram. Sample answer: The heights of the intervals vary from low to high. There are two valleys of the same height.

6c. Answers will vary and may include:
- all age groups increase except 5-19 year olds
- there is a large increase in the 25-34, 35-44, and 65 and over groups
- the median age appears to have gone up.

6d. No. When data is given in intervals, you do not have ordered pairs.

Page 32 **7a**. Sample answer: Stem-and-leaf plot will quickly show how many states have a particular percentage graduated. A histogram allows you to pick the size of the desired intervals.

7b.

HIGH SCHOOL GRADUATION RATES BY STATE, 1991

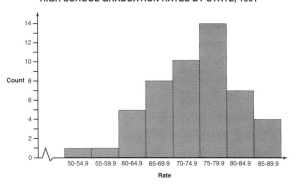

7e. Sample answer: No state graduates more than 90%. All states graduate more than 54%. Most states graduate between 70 and 79%. **7f.** Sample answer: Large urban populations; amount of state funding; socio-economic conditions.

Page 33 8.

HIGH SCHOOL DROPOUT RATES BY STATE, 1991

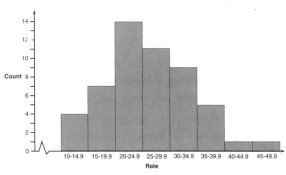

Page 36 6. Sample answer: Both sets of data have high values that make the sum of the data and thus the mean higher. When determining the median, an extremely high value does not affect it.

Page 37 12a. Roast beef. Sample answer: The median cholesterol value for roast beef is the lowest of all food types. The median should be used because of the outlier in burger cholesterol data. **12b.** Roast beef. Sample answer: The median sodium value for roast beef is also the lowest of any food type. The median should be used because of the outliers in sodium and cholesterol data for burgers. **12c.** Roast beef. Sample answer: The median fat value for roast beef is also the lowest of any of the food types. The median should be used because of the outlier in the fat data for burgers. **12d.** Roast beef. Sample answer: Using the median calorie value for the same reasons as using the median fat value, roast beef has a median of 353 calories. The only food with a lower median calorie value is chicken with 340, but chicken has a much higher median sodium value.

Page 40 20a.

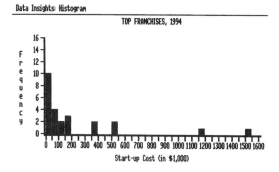

Page 41 20c. Sample answer: The graph has a high peak at the lowest values. There is a gap between 200,000 and 350,000 and between 400,000 and 500,000 and then a few more high entries. **20h.** Sample answer: The median is below the mean because there are so many entries on the low end of the graph. **20i.** Sample answer: One-half of the franchises can be started for under $76,000, while the average start-up costs are around $162,000. No business had start-up costs between $200,000 and $300,000. A few businesses have large start-up costs of over $300,000.

Page 42 21b. Sample answer: 1. Find the midpoint of each age interval. 2. Multiply these ages by the frequency. (e.g. 2.5 ◊ 17.2 = 43) 3. Compute the sum of these seven age-frequency products. 4. Compute the sum of the frequencies. 5. Divide the answer to part 3 by the answer to part 4 to obtain an approximate mean age. **21d.** Sample answer: 1. Sum the frequencies to find the total frequency. 2. Divide total frequency by 2 to obtain 1/2 of the total population. 3. Locate the interval in which the median lies by adding the frequencies of the first intervals until you are over the half-way mark. 4. Use interpolation to determine the distance into the interval for the median estimate. **21e.** mean; mean; For 1990 both the mean and median lines have moved higher compared to 1970. **21f.** Sample answer: Yes. The mean is pulled higher than the median because of the large amount of data stretched to the right.

Page 43 22c. Sample answer: They should be very close together because the graph is somewhat symmetric. **23.** Sample answer: If the histogram is symmetric around a vertical line, then that line represents the median and mean of the set of data. If the graph is skewed one direction, then the mean is pulled away from the median in the same direction. **24.** Sample answer: Of the three measures of center, mean, median, and mode, the median is the most frequent statistic choice because it is very resistant to the influence of extreme data. If the data has been ordered, it is easily located as the "center" of the data. The main disadvantages are that you must have ordered data and it does not take the actual data into account. The mean takes into account each piece of data. It is familiar to most people and easily computed. In the absence of outliers or skewed data, it is a good broad describer. The mode is easy to locate (especially on a graph) and it is used to find "most popular" type solutions. If one value in a set of data has a relatively high frequency, the mode gives a good representation of the set. The mode is not a good measure of center if its frequency is close to the frequencies of other values in the set of data.

Page 46   1c. The new mean will be the original mean increased by n degrees. The new median will be the original median increased by n degrees.   **1e.** The new mean will be the original mean decreased by n degrees. The new median will be the original median decreased by n degrees.

Page 47   6a. Sample answer: The second line plot has been stretched twice as long to the right.

Page 48   6c. The new mean will be k times the original mean. The new median will be k times the original median.
9. 60%; All the scores will be multiplied by a factor of 10, causing the data to be stretched by a factor of 10. The modal value will also be multiplied by 10.

Page 49   13e.

$$\frac{X_1 + c + X_2 + c + X_3 + c + X_4 + c + X_5 + c}{5} =$$

$$\frac{X_1 + X_2 + X_3 + X_4 + X_5 + 5c}{5} = \overline{X} + c$$

Page 50   1b. One-fourth or 25%. Taking half of half of the data points gives one-fourth or 25% of the data points.

Page 51   2. Sample answer: There is much variability in the upper quartile. Since the median is relatively close to the lower quartile, there is more variability between the minimum value and the lower quartile than between the lower quartile and the median.   **3d.** Sample answer: The lines for median, least value, and lower extreme are close together reflecting the cluster of data at the low end of the scale. The upper quartile line is a little farther to the right representing the stretch occurring in the high data. The greatest value line is far to the right reflecting the gap in the data and the outlier.

Page 52   4d. Sample answer: Approximately one-fourth of the foods have calorie values between 340 and 400.   **4f.** The upper whisker is longer so the spread of the upper 25% of the set of data is larger than the spread of the lower 25% of the set.

Page 54   6c.

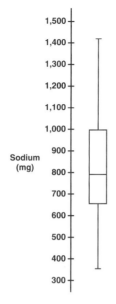

Page 55   6d. The box-and-whisker plot for salt is more symmetric. The whiskers of the box plot are close to the same length and the median for the salt content is closer to the middle of the box than the median for calories.   **7a.** The box is stretched to the greater numbers. Therefore the mean will be to the right of the median.   **7c.** Yes. Since the median is closer to the middle of the box, this means that the data is more symmetric. mean = 825.1; median = 789

8a.

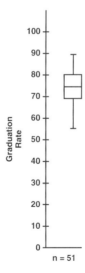

8b. The box-and-whisker plot seems more informative because the lower extreme, lower quartile, median, upper quartile, upper extreme, and range are readily available. The mean and variability can be approximated with a quick glance also. However, the box plot does not enable you to find the mode or frequency of data.

9b.

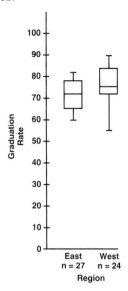

Page 56 **9c.** The West has a much higher graduation rate. In fact, the upper quartile for the East is about the same a the median for the West. Answers may vary and may include references to urban populations and poverty.   **9h.** The eastern states appear to have more variation because the interquartile range is larger.

9i.

	East	West
L.Q.	65.60	72.35
Median	73.10	76.35
U.Q.	78.50	82.95

Page 56 **10a.**

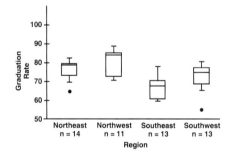

Page 57   **12a.**

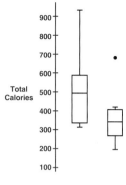

12b. Sample answer: Burgers are higher in calories and have greater variation in the number of calories. The median calories for chicken is approximately the same as the lower quartile for burgers.   **12c.** No. The box for fish is misleading. Because there are only five data points, there are no data inside the boxes. The five-number summary is sufficient.

13a.

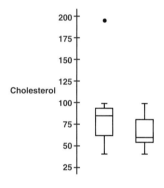

13b. Sample answer: Burgers appear to have the greatest variation because of the large IQR. Also, most burgers have a high cholesterol while most of the chicken has low cholesterol.

14a.

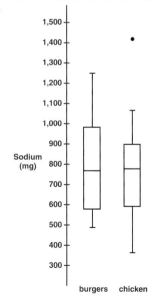

14b. Sample answers: The medians are about the same. The burger data is skewed to the high values. The burger box is larger indicating a larger spread in the distribution.

15a.

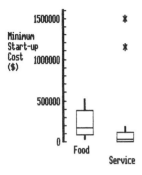

15b. Sample answers: The food industries are much more expensive to start up. They also have a large variability in start-up costs. Most service industries have extremely low start-up costs.

Page 58   16a. Sample answer:

```
251    LET D = N * 0.75
252    LET Q = (X(D) + X(D + 1))/2
253    LET G = N/4
254    LET U = (X (G) + X(G + 1))/2

260    GOTO 275

271    LET D = K * 1.5
272    LET Q = X(D)
273    LET G = K/2
274    LET U = X(G)
275    PRINT
276    PRINT "THE LOWER QUARTILE IS "; Q

291    PRINT
292    PRINT "THE UPPER QUARTILE IS "; U
```

16b. Sample answer:

```
293    PRINT "THE FIVE-NUMBER SUMMARY"
294    PRINT "FOR THIS SET OF DATA IS"
295    PRINT "LV = ";X(N)
296    PRINT "LQ = ";Q
297    PRINT "M = " ;M
298    PRINT "UQ = " ;U
299    PRINT "GV = "; X(1)
```

Page 59   1a. English. The mean for the English test is 74, and the mean for the Social Studies test is 72.   **1c.** English: 65, 68.5, 73, 76, 94   Social Studies: 45, 57.5, 73, 85.5, 100; The IQR for Social Studies is larger so it has more variability.
1d. Sample answer: Yes. The mean for English would be 72, which is the same as the mean for Social Studies. The medians remain the same so the performance is similar on the two tests.
1e. Sample answer: No. Social Studies would still have greater variability. The upper quartile and maximum are both 76 for English.

Page 60   2. Sample answers: (1) Since 94 is changed to 76, the sum is decreased by 18 units, $\frac{666-18}{9}$ .or 72 (2) $\frac{18}{9}$ = 2 so the mean decreases by 2. 74 ~ 2 =72

Page 61   4c. Sample answer: The mean deviations for temperatures in San Francisco would be smaller than Kalamazoo's mean deviation because San Franciso's temperature is more consistent throughout the year.

Page 63   8a. The S.D. for cholesterol in burgers is 40.9. The S.D. for cholesterol in chicken is 16.6. Therefore, there is greater variability in cholesterol in burgers.   **8b.** No. Without the outlier, cholesterol in burgers is 17.8, so it is still greater than the cholesterol in chicken.   **9.** The S.D. for sodium in burgers is 239.2. The S.D. for sodium in chicken is 267.1. Therefore, there is greater variability in sodium in chicken.

Page 65   10. Sample answer: The acceleration should have less variability because the range is only 9.4 while the range for the braking distance is 41. S.D. for acceleration is 2.335 seconds, and S.D. for braking distance is 11.002 feet.
11. Sample answer: Braking; The range for braking is larger than the range for EPA. S.D. for braking is 6.173 ,and S.D. for EPA is 2.826.

12a. A box-and-whisker plot will give an estimate for the summary statistics.

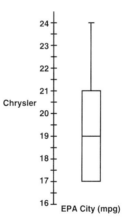

12c. Sample answer: Of the 9 models tested, the Imperial, Monaco ES, and the Premier ES Limited are tied at the low mpg of 17. The Stealth R/T Turbo has the best EPA at 24 mpg. The data cluster near 18, and the mean mpg is 19.3. There is little variation in mpg as shown by the 2.309 standard deviation.
13c. Answers will vary. Students should report means and standard deviations or medians and ranges. The mean and median represent central tendency and the range and S.D. represent the spread of the distribution.

	Ford	Chrysler	GM
Mean	19.375	19.333	19.9
S.D.	2.826	2.309	6.7
Median	18	19	17
Range	9	7	26

Page 66 **15.** No. The new design may produce differing braking effects on the various Ford automobiles. It may have improved braking distance of some models more than others.

Page 67 **18.** No. A counter example is: 2, 2, 2, 12, 12, 12 has a mean of 5 and S.D. of 5. Also, if the data are lees than 1 unit from the mean, the squaring process will make the standard deviation smaller than the mean deviation.

2.

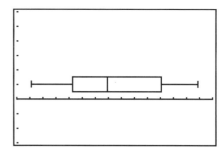

Page 69

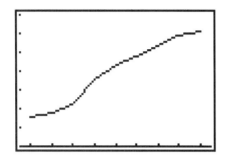

Page 70 1.

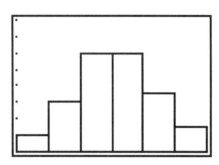

2.

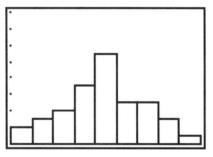

Page 71 1.

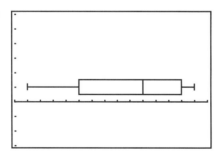

Exploring Data

An Alternative Unit
for Representing and
Analyzing One-Variable Data

GLENCOE
Mathematics Replacement Units

GLENCOE

McGraw-Hill

New York, New York
Columbus, Ohio
Mission Hills, California
Peoria, Illinois

Printed in the United States of America.

Send all inquiries to:
Glencoe/McGraw-Hill
936 Eastwind Drive
Westerville, Ohio 43081

ISBN: 0-02-824206-8 (Student Edition)
ISBN: 0-02-824207-6 (Teacher's Annotated Edition)

1 2 3 4 5 6 7 8 9 10 VH/LH-P 03 02 01 00 99 98 97 96 95 94

NEW DIRECTIONS IN THE MATHEMATICS CURRICULUM

Exploring Data is a replacement unit developed to provide an alternative to the traditional method of presentation of selected topics in Pre-Algebra, Algebra 1, Geometry, and Algebra 2.

The NCTM Board of Directors' Statement on Algebra says,
> "Making algebra count for everyone will take sustained commitment, time and resources on the part of every school district. As a start, it is recommended that local districts–...
> 3. experiment with replacement units specifically designed to make algebra accessible to a broader student population."
> (May, 1994 *NCTM News Bulletin*.)

This unit uses data analysis as a context to introduce and connect broadly useful ideas in statistics and algebra. It is organized around multi-day lessons called investigations. Each investigation consists of several related activities designed to be completed by students working together in cooperative groups. The focus of the unit is on the development of mathematical thinking and communication. Students should have access to computers with statistical software and/or calculators capable of producing graphs and lines of best fit.

About the Authors

Christian R. Hirsch is a Professor of Mathematics and Mathematics Education at Western Michigan University, Kalamazoo, Michigan. He received his Ph.D. degree in mathematics education from the University of Iowa. He has had extensive high school and college level mathematics teaching experience. Dr. Hirsch was a member of the NCTM's Commission on Standards for School Mathematics and chairman of its Working Group on Curriculum for Grades 9-12. He is the author of numerous articles in mathematics education journals and is the editor of several NCTM publications, including the *Curriculum and Evaluation Standards for School Mathematics Addenda Series, Grades 9-12*. Dr. Hirsch has served as president of the Michigan Council of Teachers of Mathematics and on the Board of Directors of the School Science and Mathematics Association. He is currently a member of the NCTM Board of Directors.

Arthur F. Coxford is a Professor of Mathematics Education and former Chairman of the Teacher Education Program at the University of Michigan, Ann Arbor, Michigan. He received his Ph.D. in mathematics education from the University of Michigan. He has been involved in mathematics education for over 30 years. Dr. Coxford is active in numerous professional organizations such as the National Council of Teachers of Mathematics, for which he was the editor of the 1988 NCTM Yearbook, *The Ideas of Algebra, K-12*. He was also the general editor of the 1993 and 1994 NCTM Yearbooks. Dr. Coxford has served as the president of the Michigan Council of Teachers of Mathematics and as the president of the School Science and Mathematics Association. He is presently the general editor of the 1995 NCTM Yearbook.

CONSULTANTS

Each of the Consultants read all five investigations. They gave suggestions for improving the Student Edition and the Teaching Suggestions and Strategies in the Teacher's Annotated Edition.

Richie Berman, Ph.D.
Teacher Education Program
University of California
Santa Barbara, California

Linda Bowers
Mathematics Teacher
Alcorn Central High School
Glen, Mississippi

William Collins
Mathematics Teacher
James Lick High School
San Jose, California

David D. Molina, Ph.D.
E. Glenadine Gibb Fellow in
  Mathematics Education &
  Assistant Professor
The University of Texas at Austin
Austin, Texas

Louise Petermann
Mathematics Curriculum Coordinator
Anchorage School District
Anchorage, Alaska

Dianne Pors
Mathematics Curriculum Coordinator
East Side Union High School
San Jose, California

Javier Solerzano
Mathematics Teacher
South El Monte High School
South El Monte, California

Table of Contents

Making Mathematics Accessible to All: First-Year Pilot Teachers

The authors would like to acknowledge the following people who field tested preliminary versions of *Exploring Data* and *Predicting with Data* in the schools indicated and whose experiences supported the development of the Teacher's Annotated Editions.

Ellen Bacon
Bedford High School
Bedford, Michigan

Elizabeth Berg
Dominican High School
Detroit, Michigan

Nancy Birkenhauer
North Branch High
    School
North Branch, Michigan

Peggy Bosworth
Plymouth Canton High
    School
Canton, Michigan

Bruce Buzynski
Ludington High School
Ludington, Michigan

Sandy Clark
Hackett Catholic Central
    High School
Kalamazoo, Michigan

Tom Duffey
Marshall High School
Marshall, Michigan

Lonney Evon
Quincy High School
Quincy, Michigan

Carole Fielek
Edsel Ford High School
Dearborn, Michigan

Stanley Fracker
Michigan Center High
    School
Michigan Center,
    Michigan

Bonnie Frye
Kalamazoo Central High
    School
Kalamazoo, Michigan

Raymond Kossakowski
East Catholic High
    School
Detroit, Michigan

William Leddy
Lamphere High School
Madison Heights,
    Michigan

Dorothy Louden
Gull Lake High School
Richland, Michigan

Michael McClain
Harry S. Truman High
    School
Taylor, Michigan

Diane Molitoris
Regina High School
Harper Woods, Michigan

Rose Martin
Battle Creek Central
    High School
Battle Creek, Michigan

Carol Nieman
Delton-Kellog High
    School
Delton-Kellog, Michigan

Beth Ritsema
Western Michigan
    University
Kalamazoo, Michigan

John Schneider
North Branch High
    School
North Branch, Michigan

Katherine Smiley
Edsel Ford High School
Dearborn, Michigan

Mark Thompson
Dryden High School
Dryden, Michigan

Paul Townsend
W.K. Kellog Middle
    School
Battle Creek, Michigan

William Trombley
Norway High School
Norway, Michigan

Carolyn White
East Catholic High
    School
Detroit, Michigan

To the Student

The most often asked question in mathematics classes must be "When am I ever going to use this?" One of the major purposes of *Exploring Data* is to provide you with a positive answer to this question.

There are several characteristics that this unit has that you may have not experienced before. Some of those characteristics are described below.

Investigations   *Exploring Data* consists of five investigations. Each investigation has one, two, or three related activities. After a class discussion introduces an investigation or activity, you will probably be asked to work cooperatively with other students in small groups as you gather data, look for patterns, and make conjectures.

Projects   A project is a long-term activity that may involve gathering and analyzing data. You will complete some projects with a group, some with a partner, and some as homework.

Portfolio Assessment   These suggest when to select and store some of your completed work in your portfolio.

Share and Summarize   These headings suggest that your class discuss the results found by different groups. This discussion can lead to a better understanding of key ideas. If your point of view is different, be prepared to defend it.

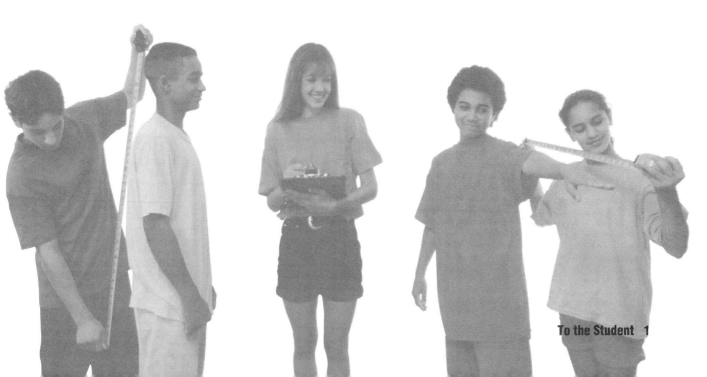

Patterns

Patterns are all around you. You hear them in the music you listen to. You see them in the clothes you wear. You experience them with the changing seasons. Observing and studying patterns is one way by which you can better understand the world in which you live. The study of patterns is the heart of mathematics.

Activity 1-1 Representing Patterns

Materials

 toothpicks

 calculator

● PARTNER PROJECT

Study the pattern of shapes below.

  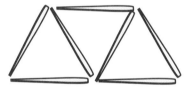

1. Use toothpicks to make the next three shapes in the pattern.

2. How many toothpicks did you use to form the fifth and sixth shapes?
   5th shape: 11 toothpicks; 6th shape: 13 toothpicks

3. How many toothpicks would be needed to form the twelfth shape?
   25 toothpicks

4. Write a sentence describing the pattern.   ***Two toothpicks that form a triangle are added at each stage.***

5. If n represents the number of toothpicks in a shape of the pattern, how could you represent the number of toothpicks in the next shape?
   n + 2

6. If the pattern was continued, would there be a shape formed by 68 toothpicks? Explain your answer.   ***No. All answers are odd because the first triangle contains 3 and 2 more are added at each stage.***

7. Recall that the distance around a shape is called its **perimeter**. If the length of a toothpick is one unit, then the perimeter of the first shape in the pattern above is 3 units.

   a. What is the perimeter of the second shape? ***4 units***

b. The table below shows the relationship of the perimeter to the number of triangles in each shape of the triangle pattern. Copy and complete the table.

Number of triangles	1	2	3	4	5	6	7	8
Perimeter in units	3	4	*5*	*6*	*7*	*8*	*9*	*10*

c. Write in words a description of how the perimeter of a shape in the pattern is related to the number of triangles. *Sample answer: The perimeter is 2 more than the number of triangles.*

Share & Summarize

d. If n represents the number of triangles in a shape of the pattern, how could you represent the perimeter of the shape? Be prepared to share your findings with the class. *n + 2*

8. The relationship between the perimeter of a shape and the number of triangles in the shape is represented by the graph shown below.

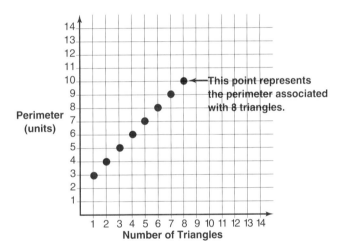

Graphing Calculator Activity

You can learn how to use a graphing calculator to plot points in Activity 1 on page 68.

a. The lowest point on the graph indicates that the first shape in the pattern has a perimeter of 3 units. Of the points shown, what does the highest point on the graph represent? *The shape consisting of 7 triangles has a perimeter of 9 units.*

b. Describe how to locate the point that represents the perimeter of a shape consisting of 8 triangles. *Sample answer: Find 8 on the horizontal axis and go up till you reach 10 on the vertical axis.*

c. Describe any pattern you see in the graph.
Sample answer: The points lie on a line.

d. Determine a method for using the pattern in the graph to find the perimeter of the shape that consists of 10 triangles. Write instructions that a classmate could use with the graph to determine the perimeter of the same shape. *Answers will vary.*

9. As you saw in Exercise 7, a table is useful for organizing data and helps in the search for patterns.

a. The table below shows the relationship of the number of toothpicks to the number of triangles in each shape of the triangle pattern. Copy and complete the table.

Number of triangles	1	2	3	4	5	6
Number of toothpicks	3	5	*7*	*9*	*11*	*13*

b. If a shape consists of 8 triangles, how many toothpicks would it contain? Verify your answer by forming the shape. *17;*

c. Write in words a description of how the number of toothpicks in a shape of the pattern is related to the number of triangles. *The number of toothpicks is 1 more than twice the number of triangles.*

d. If n represents the number of triangles in a shape of the pattern, how could you represent the number of toothpicks the shape contains? Check to see that your answer works with the data in the table.
2n + 1

e. If a shape consists of 65 triangles, how many toothpicks would it contain? *131 toothpicks*

Share & Summarize

f. If a shape in the pattern was formed using 201 toothpicks, how many triangles are in the shape? Be prepared to share your findings with the class. *100 triangles*

10. Draw a graph that shows the relationship between the number of toothpicks and the number of triangles in a shape of the pattern. Use the data from your table in Exercise 9. *See the Teacher's Answer Key.*

a. What pattern do you see in the graph?
Sample answer: The points lie on a line.

b. Describe and explain any similarities or differences between this graph and the graph in Exercise 8.
Sample answer: The points rise faster.

c. Use the pattern in the graph to determine the number of toothpicks of the shape that consists of 8 triangles. Is this the same number as your answer to Exercise 9b? *17 toothpicks. The answers are the same.*

11. Study the pattern of growing squares below.

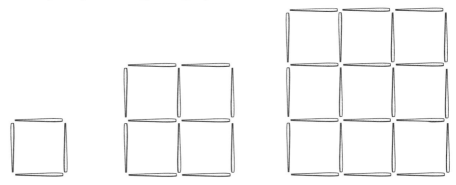

a. Describe the length of a side of each shape of the pattern. ***The length of each side increases by one from one shape to the next.***

b. Draw the next shape for the pattern. ***See the Teacher's Answer Key.***

c. If the length of a toothpick is 1 unit, then the smallest square has an area of 1 square unit. Copy and complete the table below.

Number of toothpicks on one side of the shape	1	2	3	4	5	6
Area in square units	*1*	4	*9*	*16*	*25*	*36*
Perimeter in units	*4*	8	*12*	*16*	*20*	*24*
Total number of toothpicks	*4*	12	*24*	*40*	*60*	*84*

d. If n represents the number of toothpicks on the side of a shape, how could you represent the area of the shape? ***n^2***

Share & Summarize

e. If n represents the number of toothpicks on the side of a shape, how could you represent the perimeter of the shape? Be prepared to share your findings with the class. ***4n***

12. **Extension** Refer to the pattern of squares in Exercise 11.

a. If p represents the perimeter of a shape in the pattern, how could you represent the perimeter of the ncxt shape in the pattern? ***p + 4***

b. If n represents the number of toothpicks on the side of a shape, how could you represent the total number of toothpicks in the shape? ***2n(n + 1)***

GROUP PROJECT

13. **Extension** Use toothpicks to design a pattern of triangles. Draw the shapes in the pattern. Investigate possible relationships between the number of toothpicks on a side of each shape and its perimeter and the total number of toothpicks. Write a summary of your findings. ***Sample answer: See the Teacher's Answer Key.***

Activity 1-2 Using Patterns

Materials

 tracing paper

 calculator

 pattern blocks

Careers such as that of graphics artists and designers may center around the use of patterns. The study of mathematical patterns is often helpful in their work. A **tiling pattern** is an arrangement of polygon shapes that completely covers a flat surface without overlapping or leaving gaps. The floor or ceiling in your classroom may be covered with a square tiling pattern.

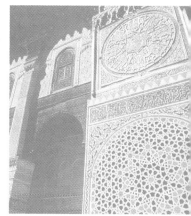

Jackie Washington, a commercial interior designer, is searching for polygon shapes that can be manufactured and used as floor tiles. Because ease of installation is a factor, she is considering only **regular polygons.** In a regular polygon, all sides are the same length, and all angles are the same size. What regular polygons could she use repeatedly by themselves to form a tiling pattern?

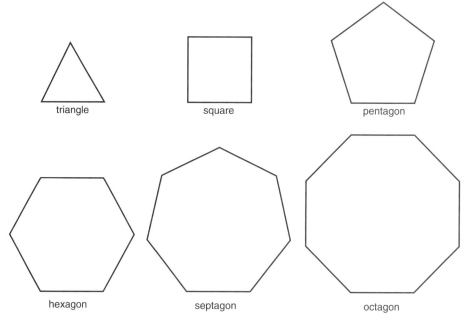

triangle   square   pentagon

hexagon   septagon   octagon

● PARTNER PROJECT

1. For each polygon above:
   a. Mark a point P on a sheet of tracing paper.
   b. Carefully trace the polygon so that P is one of the vertices.
   c. Determine whether repeated tracings of the polygon will cover the region around point P with no overlaps or gaps.
   d. Check if the pattern can be extended by repeated tracings to tile a floor.
   e. Copy and complete the table at the top of the next page.

Regular Polygon	Does the polygon form form a tiling pattern?	How many copies of the polygon fit around a point?
Triangle	*yes*	6
Square	yes	4
Pentagon	*no*	*3 +*
Hexagon	*yes*	*3*
Septagon	*no*	*2 +*
Octagon	*no*	*2 +*

f. Which of the regular polygons given could be used to form a tiling pattern?   *triangle, square, hexagon*

g. What do you think determines whether a regular polygon can be used to form a tiling?   *The measure of one angle must be a factor of 360.*

There are many other possible regular polygons. For example, a regular polygon could have 10 sides, 24 sides, or 100 sides. In order to determine which polygons could be used as floor tiles, it would be helpful if Ms. Washington had information about the size of the angles of various polygons.

2. Recall that the sum of the angles of a triangle is 180 degrees. How could you use this fact to find the sum of the angles of the pentagon shown below on the right?   *Separate the pentagon into triangles and determine the total angle measure present.*

$\angle 1 + \angle 2 + \angle 3 = 180°$ *3 triangles = 3 x 180° or 540°*

3. In a regular pentagon, all angles are **congruent**. Angles are congruent if they have the same measurement. What is the measure of any one angle of the pentagon? Explain how you determined the measure. How could you check your solution?   *540 ÷ 5 = 108; Divide the sum of the angles by the number of angles. Measure with a protractor.*

Share & Summarize

4. Copy and complete the table below using the polygons at the beginning of this activity. Be prepared to share your findings with the class.

Regular Polygon	Number of Sides	Number of Triangles	Sum of Angles	Measure of One Angle
Triangle	*3*	*1*	*180°*	*60°*
Square	4	2	360°	*90°*
Pentagon	5	3	540°	108°
Hexagon	6	4	720°	*120°*
Septagon	7	5	900°	128.57°
Octagon	8	6	1080°	135°

a. What is the least number of triangles into which a polygon of *n*-sides could be separated? ***n – 2***

b. Using patterns from the chart, what would be the sum of the angles of a regular polygon that has 20 sides? What would be the measure of any one of its angles? ***(20 – 2) x 180 = 3240°; 3240° ÷ 20 = 162°***

c. Explain in words how you would find the sum of the angles and the measure of one angle for a regular polygon with 75 sides. ***See the Teacher's Answer Key.***

d. If a regular polygon has *n* sides, how could you represent the sum of its angles? Explain your reasoning. ***(n – 2) x 180°; Answers will vary regarding the reasoning.***

e. If a regular polygon has *n* sides, how could you find the measure of one of its angles? ***[(n – 2) x 180°] ÷ n***

5. Copy the table below and use the results summarized in the two previous tables to complete it.

Regular Polygon	Is the measure of one angle a factor of 360?	Does the polygon tile?
Triangle	*yes*	*yes*
Square	yes	yes
Pentagon	*no*	*no*
Hexagon	*yes*	*yes*
Septagon	*no*	*no*
Octagon	*no*	*no*

6. A regular decagon has 10 sides. Could this shape be used repeatedly to tile a floor? Explain your reasoning. ***No, because the measure of one of its angles is 144°, which is not a factor of 360°.***

7. Under what condition(s) can a regular polygon be used to form a tiling? ***The measure of one angle must be a factor of 360°.***

Share & Summarize

8. Journal Entry Of all the regular polygons possible, which ones can be used to form tiling patterns? Be prepared to explain your reasoning to the class. ***Sample answer: See the Teacher's Answer Key.***

● HOMEWORK PROJECT

9. Make a tiling that consists of repeated use of two regular polygons. Draw a sketch of your pattern. ***Sample answer: See the Teacher's Answer Key.***

Share & Summarize

10. Journal Entry Make a list of different tiling patterns you see over the next week. Which tiling patterns seem to be most common? What might explain this? Be prepared to share your findings in class. ***Answers will vary.***

Activity 1-3 Generalizing Patterns

Materials

 centimeter cubes

 calculator

In the last part of Activity 1-1, you investigated patterns associated with square shapes formed from smaller square shapes. Suppose now that 1,000 small cubes have been stacked together and glued to form a larger cube. How many cubes would be along each edge?

If this large cube is dropped in a bucket of paint and completely submerged, how many of the small cubes will have paint on three faces? on two faces? on one face? on no faces?

In investigating these questions, you may find it helpful to collect data for specific cases and then look for a pattern.

● PARTNER PROJECT

1. Copy the table below. Use the figures below and centimeter cubes as necessary to complete the table.

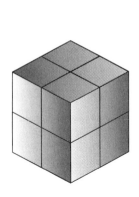 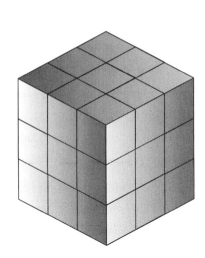 

Number of cubes along an edge	Total number of cubes	Number of cubes with paint on:			
		3 faces	2 faces	1 face	0 faces
2	8	8	0	0	0
3	27	8	12	6	1
4	64	8	24	24	8
5	125	8	36	54	27

2. Write a short paragraph describing the location on the large cube of the smaller cubes with 3 painted faces, with 2 painted faces, with 1 painted face, and with 0 painted faces. *See the Teacher's Answer Key.*

3. Suppose a large cube is formed that has six small cubes on each edge. Use your response to Exercise 2 and patterns in the table to determine:

a. the total number of cubes in this large cube *216 cubes*

b. the number of cubes with paint on 3 faces; on 2 faces; on 1 face; on 0 faces *8 cubes; 48 cubes; 96 cubes; 64 cubes*

Share & Summarize

4. Repeat Exercises 3a and 3b using a large cube having 10 small cubes along each edge. Be prepared to share your findings with the class. *Total: 1,000 cubes; 3 faces: 8; 2 faces: 96; 1 face: 384; 0 faces: 512 cubes*

5. Repeat Exercises 3a and 3b using a large cube having 20 small cubes on each edge. *Total: 8,000 cubes; 3 faces: 8 cubes; 2 faces: 216 cubes; 1 face: 1,944 cubes; 0 faces: 5,832 cubes*

6. Suppose n represents the number of small cubes along each edge of a large cube that is built and painted as described on page 9. How could you represent:

a. the total number of cubes
n^3

b. the number of cubes with paint on 3 faces
8

c. the number of cubes with paint on 2 faces
$12(n - 2)$

d. the number of cubes with paint on 1 face
$6(n - 2)^2$

e. the number of cubes with paint on 0 faces
$(n - 2)^3$

🔴 HOMEWORK PROJECT

7. Use your generalized patterns in Exercise 6 to extend the table for 7, 8, and 9 cubes along each edge of larger cubes. *See the Teacher's Answer Key.*

8. Could you build a large cube for which the entry in the "2 faces" column is 516? Explain. *Yes. 516 is divisible by 12. 12 x 43 = 516, so the number of cubes on a side is 45.*

9. Could you build a large cube for which the entry in the "1 face" column is 861? Explain. *No. $861 \div 6 = 143.4$, which is not a perfect square. So there is no whole number n such that $(n - 2)^2 = 143.4$*

10. A large cube was built for which the entry in the "0 faces" column was 571,787. What was the total number of small cubes used? *The total number of cubes used was 85^3 or 614,125.*

GROUP PROJECT

11. Draw graphs to represent: *For graphs, see the Teacher's Answer Key.*

    a. the relationship between the number of small cubes on an edge and the number of cubes with 3 painted faces.

    b. the relationship between the number of small cubes on an edge and the number of cubes with 2 painted faces.

    c. the relationship between the number of small cubes on an edge and the number of cubes with 1 painted face.

    d. the relationship between the number of small cubes on an edge and the number of cubes with 0 painted faces.

Share & Summarize

    e. Journal Entry Write a summary of patterns that you see in the graphs. Be prepared to share your findings with the class.
    Sample answer: See the Teacher's Answer Key.

12. Extension Suppose a rectangular solid is built that is 16 small cubes wide, 12 small cubes deep, and 8 small cubes high. It is then dropped in a bucket of paint and completely submerged.

    a. How many small cubes make up the larger solid? *1,536 cubes*

    b. How many of the small cubes have paint on 3 faces? on 2 faces? on 1 face? on 0 faces? *8 cubes; 120 cubes; 568 cubes; 840 cubes*

13. Extension Another rectangular solid is built and painted in a similar manner. Suppose n represents the number of cubes it is wide and that it is 5 cubes deep and 8 cubes high. How could you represent:

    a. the total number of cubes $5 \cdot 8 \cdot n$

    b. the number of cubes with paint on 3 faces   *8*

    c. the number of cubes with paint on 2 faces $4(n-2) + 4 \cdot 3 + 4 \cdot 6$

    d. the number of cubes with paint on 1 face
    $2 \cdot 3 \cdot (n-2) + 2 \cdot 6 \cdot (n-2) + 2 \cdot 3 \cdot 6$

    e. the number of cubes with paint on 0 faces $3 \cdot 6 \cdot (n-2)$

Journal

14. Journal Entry In mathematics, one often tries to understand the most general case of a problem situation such as in Exercise 6. Write the most general case situation for the problem of building and painting a rectangular solid. *See the students' work.*

15. The illustration shown below is a sequence of 1-step, 2-step, and 3-step staircases made from squares.

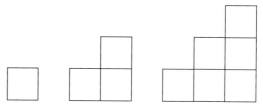

a. Write a question for your classmates that would require them to find and use a pattern for this situation. Provide a suggested solution for your question.   *Answers will vary.*

b. Write a question that would require your classmates to generalize a pattern for this situation. Write a suggested solution for your question. *Answers will vary.*

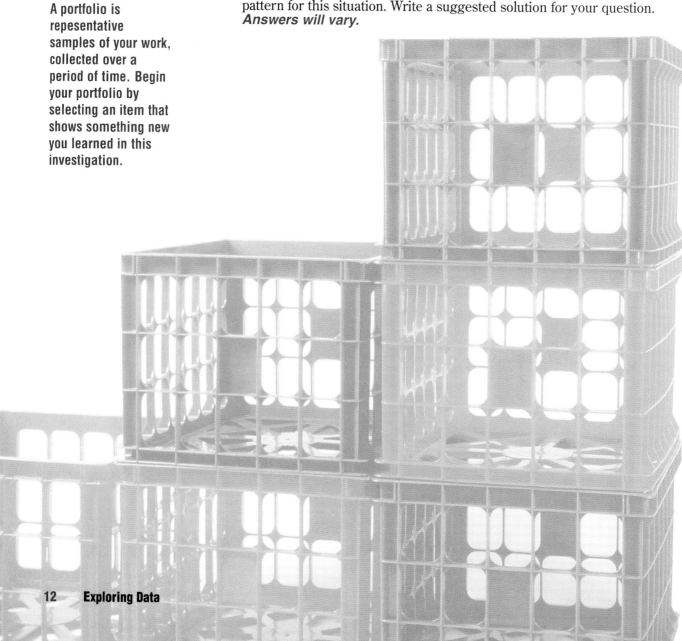

Collecting Data

Collecting and reasoning from data is a common activity in daily affairs. Data on family size is used to plan housing developments. Data on the distribution of ages in a population is used to make decisions on the development and marketing of new products. Information on traffic at intersections is used to determine the need for installation of traffic lights. Data on automobile accidents is used to determine automobile insurance rates. Data on human proportions affects the size of clothing you wear.

Decisions that are made based on data are only as good as the data itself. It is therefore very important that data collected be appropriate and accurate.

Activity 2-1 Getting to Know Yourself and Others

As you observed in completing the last investigation, these activities are designed so that you will be exploring situations and solving problems by working cooperatively in small groups. It is important that you have confidence in one another, share ideas, and help each other when asked.

You are to complete the data-gathering activities that follow by working together in groups of four. For each project, each group member is to assume a different role.

Materials

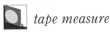 *tape measure*

 scissors

Role	Responsibility
Project Leader	Recommends data-gathering methods and units of measure appropriate for the situation.
Measurement Specialist	Performs the actual measurements as needed.
Recorder	Records measurements taken.
Quality Controller	Carefully observes the measuring and recording processes and suggests when measurements should be double-checked for accuracy.

Group Project 1

1. Select and identify the persons in your group who will be the project leader, the recorder, the measurement specialist, and the quality controller.

   a. Measure, in inches, the height and armspan of each person in your group. Record your data in a table like the one shown below.
   See students' work.

Name	Height	Armspan

   b. What one height would be most representative of your group?
   Answers will vary. Students may pick one in the middle.

   c. Do you think your representative group height would be a good representative of the entire class? Explain your reasoning.
   Answers will vary.

Share & Summarize

   d. How much variation is there in the armspans of your group?
   Answers will vary.

   e. Do you think the amount of variation in armspans of your class would be less than or greater than that in your group? Explain your reasoning.
   Sample answer: See the Teacher's Answer Key.

   f. Extend your table and combine your data for heights and armspans with that of the other groups. Check your responses to Exercises 1c and 1e. *See student's work.*

   g. On the basis of the class data, does there appear to be a relationship between height and armspan? Be prepared to explain your reasoning to the class. *Sample answer: As height increases, armspan increases.*

Group Project 2

2. Select and identify new persons in your group who will be the project leader, the recorder, the measurement specialist, and the quality controller.

a. Measure the circumference (distance around) of the thumb and wrist of each person in your group. Record your data in a table like the one shown below.

Name	Circumference	
	Thumb	Wrist

Share & Summarize

b. Extend your table and combine your data of thumb and wrist circumferences with that of the other groups.

c. On the basis of the class data, what relationship do you see between the wrist and thumb size of a person? *Sample answer: Circumference of wrist is about twice the circumference of thumb.*

d. The Lilliputians in the novel, *Gulliver's Travels*, when making clothes for Gulliver estimated, "…that twice round the thumb is once round the wrist, and so on to the neck…" Explain how you could verify this statement. *Sample answer: Collect class data on neck size and compare to wrist sizes.*

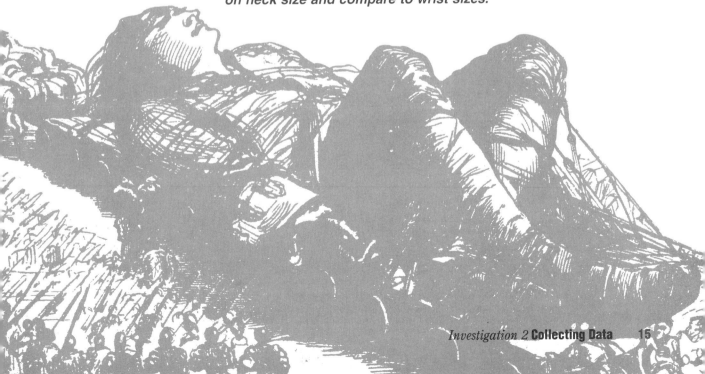

Group Project 3

3. Select and identify new persons in your group to be the project leader, the recorder, the measurement specialist, and the quality controller.

a. Determine the shoe length and stride length for each person in your group. Record the data in a table like the one shown below.

Student name	Shoe length	Stride length

b. Why do you think you were asked to determine shoe length rather than shoe size for individuals in your group? *Sample answer: Men's and women's shoes of the same size are not the same length.*

c. What is the smallest shoe length in the class? What is the largest shoe length? *Answers will vary.*

d. Compare your method for measuring stride length with that of the other groups. Agree on a common method and adjust the measurements in your table accordingly. *See student's work.*

Share & Summarize

e. Extend your table and combine your data for shoe lengths and stride lengths with that of the other groups. Use the same units of measure for all students.

Group Project 4

4. Identify the person in your group who has not been the project leader, the recorder, the measurement specialist, and the quality controller. Each person should serve in that role.

a. For each member of your group, determine the person's month of birth and whether the person is right- or left-handed. Record your data in a table like the one shown on the next page.

Name	Month of Birth	Hand Dominance (right/left)

b. On the basis of your data, estimate the number of left-handed students in your class.   *Answers will vary.*

c. Extend your table and combine your data for birthmonths and hand dominance with that of the other groups. Check your prediction in part b.

d. What percent of the girls in your class are left-handed? What percent of the boys are left-handed?   *Answers will vary.*

Share & Summarize

Portfolio Assessment

Combine the tables you made in this activity into one large table. Place this summary table in your portfolio for use in a later investigation.

e. Based on the data for your entire class, do you think the percentage of girls in your school who are left-handed is greater than, the same as, or less than the percentage of boys who are left-handed? Be prepared to explain your reasoning to the class.   *Answers will vary.*

f. What is the most frequently occurring birthmonth in your class?
   Answers will vary.

g. Does there appear to be a relationship between month of birth and hand dominance? Explain.   *Sample answer: No. They do not seem to be related.*

5. Extension   Determine the thumb dominance of a sample of your classmates by having each person fold their hands on top of a desk with fingers interlocked. The dominant thumb is the one on top. Add a column to the hand dominance table and record the appropriate thumb dominance data for each student. Does their appear to be a relationship between hand dominance and thumb dominance? Explain.   *Answers will vary.*

6. Extension   Research how eye dominance can be determined. Use this method to determine the eye dominance of a sample of your classmates. Does there appear to be a relationship between hand dominance and eye dominance? Explain your reasoning.   *See the Teacher's Answer Key.*

Journal

7. Journal Entry   How well did your group cooperate in completing this activity? Describe any problems the group experienced and how you managed them.   *See student's work.*

Displaying Data

As we move toward the 21st century, we have increasingly become an information society. Making sense of information and data is important in daily living and is a common feature of careers in industry and business – from the assembly line to the boardroom. Organizing data in tables and representing data in graphs, as you did in the last two investigations, are two methods that are often helpful in making sense of data.

Activity 3-1 Line Graphs

Materials

 graph paper

 colored pencils

The Nielson ratings provide information on the percentage of U.S. households with televisions that are tuned into various programs. These ratings are used by the networks in determining the cost of television commercials.

The **double line graph** below shows average per game Nielson ratings for NFL and college football televised between 1980 and 1990. The rating of 17.6 for NFL games in 1980 means that on the average 17.6% of all households with televisions watched NFL games.

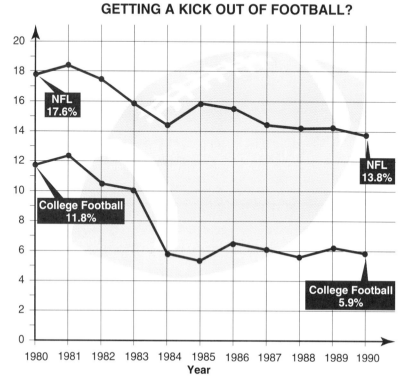

Source: Detroit Free Press, May 12, 1992

Group Project

1. a. In what year did the NFL have its highest rating? *1981*

b. In what year did the NFL have its lowest rating? *1990*

c. Estimate the Nielson rating for NFL games in 1986. *approximately 15.7%*

d. In what years did the NFL show an increase in ratings from the previous year? *1981, 1985, and possibly 1989*

e. For how many years during the period 1980-1990 were the Nielson ratings for NFL games above 15? *6 years*

f. Overall, what trend do you see in NFL viewing over the period 1980-1990? *NFL viewing is gradually decreasing.*

2. a. In what year did college football have its highest rating? *1981*

b. In what year did college football have its lowest rating? *1985*

c. In what years did college football show an increase in ratings from the previous year? *1981, 1986, 1989*

d. Estimate the Nielson rating for college football games in 1986. *approximately 6.7%*

e. In what year did college football ratings experience their sharpest decline? *1984*

f. Overall, what trend do you see in college football viewing over the period 1980-1990? *College football viewing decreased overall.*

g. What, if anything, can you say about college football viewership in 1995? Explain your reasoning. *Answers will vary.*

3. Did the NFL or college football suffer the greater loss of television viewership during the 1980s? Explain the basis for your conclusion.
Sample answer: College football had a greater loss of viewership. There was an overall drop of approximately 4% in NFL viewership and 6% in college viewership.

4. What are some possible reasons for the decline in television viewership of football? *Answers will vary. Possible reasons could include: the NFL players' strike of 1984; an overlap of sport seasons; availability of cable television; ESPN.*

The double line graph below shows average per game Nielson ratings for college and professional basketball during the period 1980-1990.

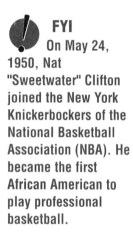

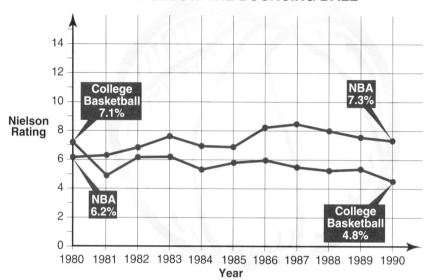

FOLLOW THE BOUNCING BALL

Source: Detroit Free Press, May 12, 1992

5. a. Which had the greater share of the viewing audience in 1980, college basketball or the NBA? *college*

b. Which of the two levels of basketball, professional or college, had the greater share of the viewing audience in 1990? *professional*

6. a. In what years did college basketball show a decrease in ratings from the previous year? *1981, 1984, 1987, 1988, 1990*

b. In what years did the NBA show a decrease in ratings from the previous year? *1984, 1988, 1989, 1990*

7. a. Overall, what trend do you see in NBA viewing over the period 1980-1990? *Overall, there was a slight increase in viewing.*

b. What might explain this trend? *Answers will vary, popularity of super stars might be one explanation.*

8. What percent of its 1980 audience was lost by college basketball during the period 1980-1990? *2.3%*

9. Overall, how does the trend in ratings of college basketball viewership compare to the ratings of college football viewership? Be prepared to explain your reasoning to the class. *See the Teacher's Answer Key.*

 **Share & Summarize**

Line graphs are useful in representing and analyzing how a quantity changes with respect to time. Time is usually represented along the **horizontal axis**. Values that the quantity may take on are then represented along the **vertical axis**. It is important that the axes are labeled.

The table below lists average Nielson ratings for network televised broadcasts of individual sports for the years 1980-1990.

Nielson Rationgs for Individual Sports											
	'80	'81	'82	'83	'84	'85	'86	'87	'88	'89	'90
Auto Racing	3.1	6.5	5.4	6.1	5.6	4.2	4.7	4.3	3.8	4.4	4.1
Bowling	8.1	7.5	7.5	6.6	5.6	5.1	5.1	4.7	3.9	4.1	3.6
Golf	4.5	4.9	4.9	5.0	4.5	4.5	4.1	4.1	3.4	3.6	3.4
Boxing	9.8	9.0	5.3	5.8	3.8	4.8	3.1	3.4	2.7	3.5	3.3
Tennis	2.9	2.6	2.9	3.5	3.4	3.8	3.2	2.9	3.1	3.5	3.1
Horse Racing	8.6	13.8	8.2	8.2	6.9	4.4	6.7	6.0	4.0	3.7	2.4

Source: Detroit Free Press, May 12, 1992

● HOMEWORK PROJECT 1

10. Copy the grid shown below onto a sheet of grid paper.

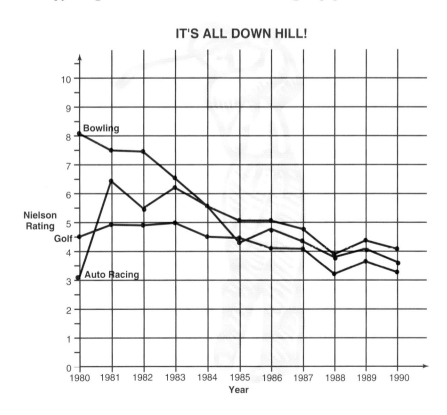

Graphing Calculator Activity

You can learn how to use a graphing calculator to make a line graph in Activity 2 on page 69.

a. Draw and label a line graph for ratings of auto racing viewership.
See students' work. Sample answer is shown above.

b. Using a different color pen or pencil, draw and label a line graph for bowling viewership on the same grid.   *See students' work. Sample answer is shown on page 21.*

c. Using a third color pen or pencil, draw and label a line graph for golf viewership on the same grid.   *See students' work. Sample answer is shown on page 21.*

11. a. Which had the highest rating in 1980, auto racing, bowling, or golf ? Did you refer to the table or your graph?   *Bowling; Answers will vary.*

b. Which of the three sports had the highest rating in 1990?
Auto Racing

c. Which of the three sports showed the greatest change in ratings over the period 1980-1990? Did you refer to the table or your graph? Why?   *Bowling; Answers will vary.*

d. Which of the sports had the highest rating during the period? What was the rating? When did it occur? Did you refer to the table or your graph? Why?   *Bowling; 8.1; 1980; Answers will vary.*

● PARTNER PROJECT

12. On a sheet of grid paper, prepare a grid that you can use to draw line graphs of television ratings of boxing, tennis, and horse racing during the period 1980-1990.

a. Label the horizontal and vertical axes properly.   *See students work.*

b. Draw and label a line graph for boxing viewership.   *See the Teacher's Answer Key.*

c. Using a different color pen or pencil, draw and label a line graph for tennis viewership.   *See the Teacher's Answer Key.*

d. Using a third color pen or pencil, draw and label a line graph for horse racing viewership.   *See the Teacher's Answer Key.*

13. a. Which showed an overall increase in ratings during the period 1980-1990, boxing, tennis, or horse racing? Did you refer to the table or your graph? Why?   *Tennis; Answers will vary.*

b. Which of these three sports showed the greatest overall loss in ratings during the period? Did you refer to the table or your graph? Why?
Boxing; Answers will vary.

c. In what year(s) were the ratings for horse racing at least double the ratings for boxing? Did you refer to the table or your graph? Why?
1986; Answers will vary.

d. Were there any years in the period 1980-1990 for which two of the sports shared the same rating? If so, what were the sports and what were the years? Did you refer to the table or your graph in answering these questions? Why?   *Yes; boxing and tennis, 1989; Answers will vary.*

14. Compare all six of your line graphs. For which individual sport did the ratings fluctuate the most? Be prepared to explain your reasoning to the class.   *Horse racing*

Homework Project 2

Journal

15. Journal Entry   Write a short paragraph that compares the overall changes for television ratings of team sports with those of individual sports during the period 1980-1990.   *Sample answer: Team sports ratings did not fluctuate as much as individual sports ratings in the 1980's.*

16. Extension   Study the multiple line graph shown below.

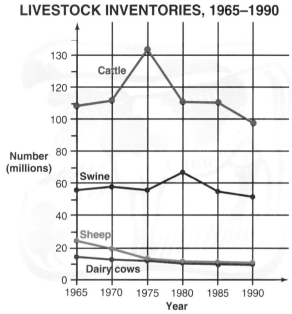

LIVESTOCK INVENTORIES, 1965–1990

Source: U.S. Bureau of the Census, Statistical Abstact of the United States 1994

a. Write a paragraph that describes and compares the trends in livestock population as displayed by the graphs.   *See the Teacher's Answer Key.*

b. How might you explain the pattern of cattle and swine inventories across the period 1965-1990?   *Answers will vary.*

c. What would be a reasonable estimate of the number of swine in 1977?   *60 million*

d. Make a table of livestock inventory numbers (in millions) by census years. You will need to estimate the numbers.   *See the Teacher's Answer Key.*

e. Why do you think the information is provided in graph form rather than in a table?   *Sample answer: A graph quickly shows which production is larger at any time. It is also easier to read changes in production and see overall changes. Comparisons can be made quicker on a graph.*

Activity 3—2   Stem-and-Leaf Plots

As a society, the United States has become increasingly health conscious. People are exercising more and watching what they eat. The table below gives nutritional information on fast foods. Total calories, amount of fat in grams, amount of cholesterol in milligrams, and amount of sodium (salt) in milligrams are provided. Foods are organized according to meat type: burgers, chicken, fish, roast beef, and turkey.

FYI
The first McDonald's restaurant opened April 15, 1955 in Des Plaines, Illinois.

How Fast Foods Compare

Company	Fast food	Total calories	Fat (g)	Cholesterol (mg)	Sodium (mg)
McDonald's	McLean Deluxe	320	10	60	670
Wendy's	Single (plain)	340	15	65	500
McDonald's	Quarter Pounder	410	20	85	650
McDonald's	Big Mac	500	26	100	890
Burger King	Hamburger Deluxe	344	19	43	496
Wendy's	Big Classic	570	33	90	1,085
Burger King	Whopper	614	36	90	865
Hardee's	Big Deluxe Burger	500	30	70	760
Burger King	Double Whopper w/Cheese	935	61	194	1,245
Hardee's	Grilled Chicken	310	9	60	890
Hardee's	Chicken Fillet	370	13	55	1,060
Wendy's	Grilled Chicken	340	13	60	815
Wendy's	Chicken (regular)	430	19	60	725
Burger King	BK Broiler Chicken	379	18	53	764
McDonald's	McChicken	415	20	42	770
McDonald's	Chicken McNuggets (6)	270	15	56	580
Burger King	Chicken Sandwich	685	40	82	1,417
Kentucky Fried Chicken	Lite'n Crispy (4 pieces)	198	12	60	354
Kentucky Fried Chicken	Original Recipe(4 pieces)	248	15	90	575
Kentucky Fried Chicken	Extra Crispy (4 pieces)	324	21	99	638
Hardee's	Fisherman's Fillet	500	24	70	1,030
McDonald's	Filet-O-Fish	370	18	50	930
Burger King	Ocean Catch Fish Filet	495	25	57	879
Wendy's	Fish Fillet Sandwich	460	25	55	780
Arby's	Fish Fillet	537	29	79	994
Arby's	French Dip	345	12	47	678
Arby's	Regular Roast Beef	353	15	39	588
Arby's	Super Roast Beef	529	28	47	798
Hardee's	Turkey Club	390	16	70	1,280
Arby's	Turkey Deluxe	399	20	39	1,047

Source: Hope Health Letter, Fall 1991

PARTNER PROJECT

1. Why might people concerned about health prefer low-calorie, low-fat, low-cholesterol, low-salt foods? *Sample answer: So they could keep their weight down and have lower blood pressure and cholesterol levels.*

2. An examination of the entries of any column of the table reveals that there is considerable **variation**. Which of the four variables – total calories, fat, cholesterol, or sodium – shows the greatest variation? Explain your reasoning. *Sodium, because it has the greatest spread of values (354 to 1,417).*

3. The pattern of variation for a measure such as calories is best seen in a graph. A special graph, called a **stem-and-leaf plot**, displays data in a way that allows you to see variation quickly.

   The beginning of a stem-and-leaf plot of the total calorie data is shown below.

   ```
                    1 | 98
                    2 | 48 70
                    3 | 10 20 24 40 40 44 45 63 70 70 79 90 99
                    4 | 10 15 30 60 95        ← leaves
      stems →       5 | 00 00 00 29 37 70
                    6 | 14 85
                    7 |
                    8 |
                    9 | 35                        4|10 = 410
   ```

   The line   4 | 10 15 30 60 95   represents the data for McDonald's Quarter Pounder and McChicken, Wendy's Chicken (regular) and Fish Fillet Sandwich, and Burger King's Ocean Catch Fish Filet, respectively. Note that the leaves were arranged in increasing order from left to right. You may find it easiest to first record the leaves as they appear in the table of data and then reorder them as necessary. Copy and finish this stem-and-leaf plot. *See plot above. (Note: You may wish to have students use graph paper to keep the stems lined up vertically.)*

4. Study your completed stem-and-leaf plot.

   a. What is the least number of calories? What is the greatest number of calories? Which fast food items are associated with these values? *198; 935; Lite'n Crispy Chicken, Double Whopper with Cheese*

   b. Estimate the center of this distribution of total calorie data. Explain how you determined the estimate. *Answers will vary. There are 30 entries. The middle is between the fifteenth and sixteenth entries or approximately 395.*

c. What overall pattern do you see in the plot? Does the plot have one or more peaks? ***Most of the data are clustered in the 300-600 range; One peak***

d. Does the plot appear symmetric? If not, does the plot appear to be stretched more to the higher or lower number of total calories? ***No. It appears to be stretched to the higher calories.***

e. Do you see any gaps in the overall pattern of the plot? Are there any exceptions to the overall pattern? ***Yes, there are no 700 or 800 calorie entries; yes, 935***

5. In what ways is the stem-and-leaf plot better than the table for displaying the data on calories? In what ways is it worse? ***See the Teacher's Answer Key.***

6. a. Stem-and-leaf plots were created to provide a quick way to visualize patterns in data. Usually it is easy and common to use single-digit leaves. In the case of the total calorie data, this can be accomplished by dropping the last digit of each entry. For example, 320 becomes 32 and 248 becomes 24. Create a stem-and-leaf plot by following this format. Remember that the stems are still hundreds of calories, but the leaves are now tens of calories rather than units or ones. ***See the Teacher's Answer Key.***

b. How does the shape of this plot compare with the plot you made in Exercise 3? ***They are the same.***

c. What are the advantages of making stem-and-leaf plots with leaves consisting of only a single digit? What are the disadvantages? ***Sample answers: less space used, easier to read; less accurate.***

7. a. Make a stem-and-leaf plot for the fat content of the fast foods in the table on page 24. ***See the Teacher's Answer Key.***

b. Write a paragraph summary of the information you can see from looking at the plot. You will find the questions in Exercise 4 to be a helpful guide. ***See the Teacher's Answer Key.***

c. Rotate the stem-and-leaf plot of the fat content 90° counterclockwise. Do the same for the stem-and-leaf plot of the calorie data. Which set of data appears to have greater variation? Explain your reasoning. ***The calorie data because it has a greater spread and larger gap.***

 **Share & Summarize**

8. If you were to make a stem-and-leaf plot with single digit leaves of the sodium contents of fast foods, how would you record 496? 1,085? Be prepared to explain the basis for your method to the class. ***Sample answer: Record 496 as 4 | 9 and 1,085 as 10 | 8. The stem stands for hundreds and the leaf stands for the tens. 4 | 9 = 490 and 10 | 8 = 1,080.***

HOMEWORK PROJECT

The table below gives, in alphabetical order, the rental income of the top 25 videos in 1994.

Top Video Rentals	Income
Home Alone 2: Lost in New York (20th Century-Fox)	$102,000,000
Batman Returns (Warner Brothers)	100,100,000
Lethal Weapon 3 (Warner Brothers)	80,000,000
Sister Act (Buena Vista)	62,420,000
Aladdin (Buena Vista)	60,000,000
Wayne's World (Paramount)	54,000,000
A League of Their Own (Columbia)	53,100,000
Basic Instinct (TriStar)	53,000,000
The Bodyguard (Warner Brothers)	52,900,000
A Few Good Men (Columbia)	52,000,000
Bram Stoker's Dracula (Columbia)	47,200,000
The Hand That Rocks the Cradle (Buena Vista)	39,334,000
Patriot Games (Paramount)	37,500,000
Fried Green Tomatoes (Universal)	37,402,827
Unforgiven (Warner Brothers)	36,000,000
White Men Can't Jump (20th Century-Fox)	34,115,000
Boomerang (Paramount)	34,000,000
Under Siege (Warner Brothers)	33,000,000
Alien 3 (20th Century-Fox)	31,762,000
The Last of the Mohicans (20th Century-Fox)	31,491,000
Death Becomes Her (Universal)	30,433,483
Beauty and the Beast (continuing run)	30,415,000
Housesitter (Universal)	30,390,622
Far and Away (Universal)	28,910,698
Honey, I Blew Up the Kid (Buena Vista))	27,417,000

Source: Information Please Almanac, 1994

9. a. Decide what you would use as the stems of a stem-and-leaf plot of this data. Decide what you would use as the leaves. ***See students' work.***

b. Make a stem-and-leaf plot based on your decisions. ***See the Teacher's Answer Key.***

 **Journal**

c. Journal Entry Write a paragraph summary of the information you can see from looking at the plot. ***Answers may vary.***

10. Extension What kind(s) of breakfast cereal do you eat? Poll the other members of the class on this question. Visit a supermarket and, for each cereal, record the amount of calories and the amount of sugar (in grams) in a serving. Check the serving size. It may be different from cereal to cereal. Only use cereals with the same serving size.

    a. Make a stem-and-leaf plot of the calorie data. Write a paragraph summary of the information you see from looking at the plot. *See students' work.*

    b. Make a stem-and-leaf plot of the sugar data. Write a summary of the information conveyed by the plot. *See students' work.*

    c. Compare the two stem-and-leaf plots. What do you notice? *See the Teacher's Answer Key.*

11. Extension Roger Maris, a former New York Yankee, holds the record for the most home runs in one season (61). Below is a stem-and-leaf plot of the number of home runs he hit in each of his 10 years in baseball.

	Ruth		Maris	
		0	8	
		1	3 4 6	
	5 2	2	3 6 8	
	5 4	3	3 9	
9 7 6 6 6 1	1	4		
	9 4 4	5		
	0	6	1	6	1 = 61

    a. The table below shows the number of home runs Babe Ruth hit during each year of his career with the Yankees.

Year	1920	'21	'22	'23	'24	'25	'26	'27	'28	'29	'30	'31	'32	'33	'34
Home runs	54	59	35	41	46	25	47	60	54	46	49	46	41	34	22

Source: The Baseball Encyclopedia

Copy the Maris stem-and-leaf plot. Add a vertical rule to the left of the stems. Using these same stems, on the left make a stem-and-leaf plot of the home run data for Babe Ruth. *Answer is shown above.*

    b. Use this **back-to-back stem-and-leaf plot** to compare the overall performance of Maris and Ruth. *Sample answer: Overall, Ruth hit more home runs more frequently.*

Activity 3–3   Histograms

Materials

 ruler

 software

 newspapers/ magazines

Stem-and-leaf plots can be used to get a quick visual display of data from which patterns may be observed. They are most useful when the data sets are relatively small, usually 30 items or less. A special kind of bar graph called a **histogram**, can be used to display almost any number of data items.

● PARTNER PROJECT

1. To make a histogram of the calorie data for fast foods in the table on page 24, first divide the range of the data into equal parts. Here the data ranges from 198 to 935 calories. A reasonable range would be 0 to 1000 calories. This could be divided into 10 equal intervals of 100 calories each.

   a. Copy and complete the **frequency table** shown below.

Interval	Tally	Frequency
0-99		*0*
100-199	|	1
200-299	||	2
300-399	⊦⊦⊦⊦⊦⊦⊦ |||	*13*
400-499	⊦⊦⊦⊦	*5*
500-599	⊦⊦⊦⊦ |	*6*
600-699	| |	2
700-799		*0*
800-899		*0*
900-999	|	*1*

   b. You can use your completed frequency table to construct a histogram of the data. The horizontal axis represents the calorie intervals. The vertical axis represents the number or frequency of items in an interval. A rectangle whose height is the frequency of a given interval is then drawn. Copy and complete the histogram shown below.

FAST FOOD ENTREES

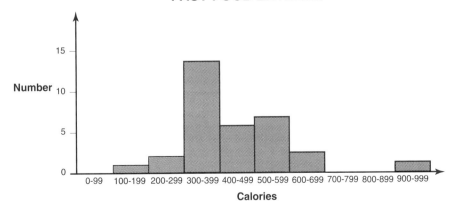

Journal

2. **Journal Entry**   Write a paragraph summary of the pattern of the data that you can see from the histogram. Consider such things as spread, location of center, symmetry, gaps, and exceptions to the pattern.
   See the Teacher's Answer Key.
3. The first step in drawing a histogram is deciding on the number and size of the intervals to use.

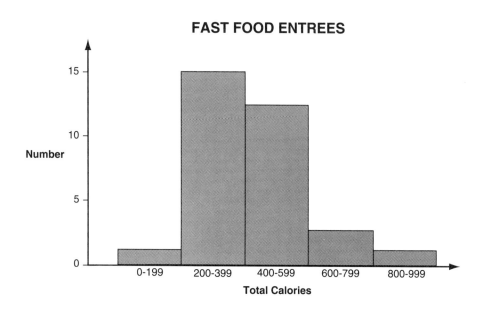

FAST FOOD ENTREES

a. What is the size of the intervals of the histogram above?
   200 calories
b. Is this histogram an accurate representation of the original data on total calories of fast foods? Explain your reasoning.   *Yes. The data, when tallied by 200 calorie intervals, gives this histogram.*
c. Is this histogram more or less informative than the histogram you made? Why?   *Not as informative. There are fewer groups so we don't notice the gap and the single high value.*
4. Compare your histogram for the calorie data with the stem-and-leaf plot you made of the same data. It will help if you first rotate the stem-and-leaf plot 90° counterclockwise. How are they similar in the information they convey? How are they different?   *The histogram and stem-and-leaf are similar in spread, gaps, peaks, and exceptions. The stem-and-leaf plot allows for more detailed information such as the center value, or maximum and minimum values.*

5. a. Make a frequency table and histogram for the data on the amount of fat in fast foods in the table on page 24. *See the Teacher's Answer Key.*

b. Does this graph display the same kind of information about the distribution of fat as did your stem-and-leaf plot of the same data? Be prepared to explain your reasoning to the class.
Yes. The shape is the same, so you can readily see gaps, clustering, peaks, and the number of items in an interval. (See exercise 4.)

● HOMEWORK PROJECT

6. The following table gives information on the make-up of the population of the United States in 1970 and in 1990.

Population (in millions)	1970	1990
Under 5 years old	17.2	18.8
5-19 years old	59.9	53.0
20-24 years old	16.4	19.1
25-34 years old	24.9	43.2
35-44 years old	23.1	37.4
45-64 years old	41.8	46.2
65 years old and over	20.0	31.1

Source: U.S. Bureau of the Census, Statistical Abstract of the United States, 1994

For answers to 6a-6d, see the Teacher's Answer Key.

a. Make a histogram for the 1970 population distribution. Describe the main features of the distribution.

b. Make a histogram for the 1990 population distribution. Describe the main features of this distribution.

c. Compare your two histograms. What are the most important changes in the U.S. age distribution during the period 1970-1990?

d. Would it have been better to represent this data by line graphs? Explain your reasoning.

7. The graduation rate (in percent) for public high schools is given below for each state and the District of Columbia.

Graphing Calculator Activity

You can learn how to use a graphing calculator to make histograms in Activity 3 on page 70.

High School Graduation Rates by State, 1991

State	Rate	State	Rate	State	Rate
Alabama	65.6	Kentucky	70.0	North Dakota	86.7
Alaska	72.3	Louisiana	54.3	Ohio	72.3
Arizona	72.4	Maine	79.0	Oklahoma	75.5
Arkansas	76.6	Maryland	73.1	Oregon	71.6
California	67.7	Massachusetts	79.7	Pennsylvania	78.5
Colorado	74.5	Michigan	69.9	Rhode Island	73.6
Connecticut	78.6	Minnesota	89.5	South Carolina	61.2
Delaware	68.0	Mississippi	61.7	South Dakota	84.2
D.C.	59.5	Misouri	72.5	Tennesee	67.8
Florida	61.2	Montana	84.9	Texas	65.9
Georgia	64.0	Nebraska	86.3	Utah	79.0
Hawaii	76.1	Nevada	77.4	Vermont	80.9
Idaho	79.7	New Hampshire	76.2	Virginia	73.6
Illinois	77.5	New Jersey	82.1	Washington	73.1
Indiana	75.3	New Mexico	69.5	West Virginia	77.5
Iowa	85.9	New York	64.4	Wisconsin	82.5
Kansas	81.1	North Carolina	68.4	Wyoming	81.7

Source: World Almanac, 1994

a. What type of graphical display do you think would be best to represent this data? Explain the basis for your reasoning. ***See the Teacher's Answer Key.***

b. Most statistical software packages will produce line graphs, stem-and-leaf plots, and histograms after you enter the data. Some graphing calculators also will produce line graphs and histograms. Use one of these tools to display the graph you proposed in part a. If possible, print a copy of your graph. ***See the Teacher's Answer Key.***

c. What is the rate of graduation in your state? How does this compare with other states? ***Answers will vary.***

d. How many states have graduation rates above 85%? ***4***

e. What conclusions can you draw from your graph? ***See the Teacher's Answer Key.***

f. What are some possible reasons why states differ in graduation rates? ***See the Teacher's Answer Key.***

g. Find out the rate of graduation at your high school. How does this rate compare with the graduation rate for your state? ***Answers will vary.***

8. **Extension** Because of the importance of education to the strength of our nation's workforce, the U.S. Department of Education also monitors dropout rates. Using only your histogram of graduation rates, sketch what you think a histogram of dropout rates for the 50 states and the District of Columbia would look like. *Sample answer: See the Teacher's Answer Key.*

9. **Extension** Most computer software that display histograms automatically select the size of the intervals. However, they also give you the option of specifying the size of the intervals. Use this customizing feature to explore the effects of different interval sizes for a histogram of the graduation rate data. Print a copy of the graph that you think best represents the data. Below the graph, explain the reason(s) for your choice of the interval size. *Answers will vary.*

GROUP PROJECT

10. **Extension** Histograms are frequently used in magazines and newspapers to convey information visually. Collect an example of a histogram that is nearly symmetric. Locate a histogram that is "double-peaked." Find a histogram that appears stretched more to the right; another that is stretched more to the left. For each histogram, note the source. *Answers will vary.*

11. Refer to your class data table you made in Investigation 2. Each member of your group should select a different variable from among the variables: height, armspan, shoe length, and stride length.

   a. Produce an appropriate graphical display of the data for the variable you selected. *See students' work.*

   b. Explain why you chose the particular kind of graph you did. *Answers will vary.*

   c. Write a paragraph summary of the information you can see from looking at the graph. *Answers will vary.*

   d. Explain to the other members of your group the conclusions you have drawn from the data for the variable you selected. Answer questions group members may have about the data and your interpretations. *Answers will vary.*

Share & Summarize

Portfolio Assessment

Select some of your work from this investigation that shows how you used a calculator or computer. Place it in your portfolio.

Describing Data

The first step in examining data is to prepare an appropriate graph. Graphical displays can help you see the overall shape of a distribution. They also can help you detect possible patterns in the data. The back-to-back stem-and-leaf plot below shows the distribution of calories in two kinds of fast foods—burgers and chicken.

Calories	
Burgers	**Chicken**
320	310
340	370
410	340
500	430
344	379
570	415
614	270
500	685
935	198
	248
	324

Burgers			Chicken
		1	9
		2	4 7
4 4 2		3	1 2 4 7 7
1		4	1 3
7 0 0		5	
1		6	8
		7	
		8	
3		9	

6 | 8 = 680

How do the shapes of the distributions compare? In general, are there more calories in a burger or in chicken? Answering the second question can be aided by the use of numerical tools for describing data.

Activity 4-1 Measures of Center

Materials

 ruler

 calculator

software

● PARTNER PROJECT

1. Since stem-and-leaf plots arrange data in increasing order, you can use the plot as an aid in searching the table for the *least* and *greatest* values. The difference between the greatest and least values of a set of data is called the **range**. For burgers, the range of calories is 935 − 320 or 615. What is the range of calories for chicken? **487**

2. The range of calories in burgers is higher than the range of calories in chicken. But the range does not provide enough information to determine whether burgers or chicken have, in general, more calories. Statistics that report the center of each set of data would be more helpful. These are

called **measures of center**. One such statistic is the **median**—the value in an ordered set of data such that half of the values are at or below it, and half are at or above it. Informally you may have been finding the median when describing the center of plots.

In the case of burgers, there are 9 values. So the median would be the fifth value in the ordered list. The median number of calories in burgers is 500. There are four values below 500 and four values above 500.

320   340   344   410   **500**   500   570   614   935

On a sheet of notebook paper, create a chart like the one shown below. What is the median number of calories in chicken? Record this statistic in the summary chart. In general, which of these two fast foods has the greater number of calories? *340; burgers*

As you calculate other statistics for the fast foods data in this activity, record your results in this chart for future reference.

Fast Food	Statistic	Calories	Fat	Cholestrol	Sodium
Burgers	Range	615			
	Median	500			
	Mean				
	Mode				
Chicken	Range				
	Median				
	Mean				
	Mode				
Fish	Range				

3. To determine the median for a set of data, the data must first be ordered from least to greatest. Refer to the data on fast foods given on page 24. In general, are there more calories in the fish or chicken fast foods? Explain your reasoning. *Sample answer: Fish. The median for fish is 495, while the median for chicken is 340.*

4. Using the data on fast foods, in general, is there more sodium (salt) in burgers or chicken? in burgers or fish? in chicken or fish? Explain your reasoning. *Sample answer: Chicken; fish; fish; The median for fish is 930. The median for chicken is 764. The median for burgers is 760.*

5. The most common measure of center is the **mean**. The Nielson ratings of televised sports programs you investigated in Activity 3-1 were based on this measure of center. To determine the mean of a set of data, you find the sum of the values in the set and then divide by the number of values in the set.

The mean number of calories in burgers is:

$($ 320 $+$ 340 $+$ 344 $+$ 410 $+$ 500 $+$ 500 $+$ 570 $+$ 614 $+$ 935 $)$ $\div$ 9 $=$ *503.6666667* or approximately 503.7.

Determine the mean number of calories in the chicken fast foods.
360.8 calories

6. For both burgers and chicken, the mean number of calories was greater than the median number of calories. How might you explain this fact?
See the Teacher's Answer Key.

7. Determine the mean number of calories in fish. How does this compare with the median number of calories in fish? Is this result consistent with your observation in Exercise 6? If not, how might you explain the difference? ***Mean = 472.4; median = 495; yes***

8. Suppose, in the listing of burgers, that the Burger King Double Whopper with Cheese was replaced by the Burger King Double Whopper with 825 calories.

    a. How would this change affect the range of calories for burgers?
    The range drops 110 calories to become 505.

    b. How would this change affect the median number of calories for burgers? ***The median does not change.***

    c. How would this change affect the mean number of calories for burgers?
    The mean would decrease by 110/9 or approximately 12 calories.

9. An **outlier** is a value in a set of data that appears to be an exception to the overall pattern of the set.

    a. In general, how do outliers affect the mean of a set of data?
    Sample answer: Outliers pull the mean value in their direction.

    b. How do outliers affect the median of a set of data? ***Outliers do not affect the median.***

10. A third measure of center is the **mode**. A mode of a set of data is the value that occurs most often in the set. The mode of the number of calories in burgers is 500. There is no mode for the total calories in the chicken fast foods data.

Refer to the fast foods data on page 24. Look at the data on the amount of fat in various fast foods. Which food types have modes for fat content? What are these values? ***Fish; Mode = 25. Chicken; Mode = 13 and 15.***

Share & Summarize

11. Would modes of grams of fat be a good basis on which to compare the fat contents of the chicken and fish selections? Be prepared to explain your reasoning to the class. ***No; The modes of fat for chicken are 13 and 15. Neither are representative of the entire set of data.***

GROUP PROJECT

12. Answer the following questions based on the fast foods data. You will find the summary chart you made for Exercise 2 helpful.
See the Teacher's Answer Key for answers to a-d.

a. If your doctor recommended a low-cholesterol diet, which of the fast food types— burgers, chicken, fish, roast beef, or turkey—would you select? Explain your reasoning and your choice of measure of center.

b. If your doctor recommended a low-cholesterol and low-salt diet, which of the fast food types would you select? Again, explain your reasoning and choice of measure of center.

c. If your doctor recommended a low-cholesterol and low-fat diet, which of the fast food types would you select? Explain your reasoning and choice of measure of center.

Share & Summarize

d. If your doctor recommended a low calorie, low-fat, and low-cholesterol diet, which of the fast food types should you select? Be prepared to explain your reasoning to the class.

13. a. Determine the mean number of calories in all 30 of the fast foods.
429.3

b. Which fast food types have a mean number of calories below the overall mean number of calories?
Turkey, roast beef, and chicken

14. When there is an even number of values in a set of data, as in the case of the total calorie data for fast foods, there is no middle number. There are two middle numbers. By examining your answer to Exercise 3 on page 25, you should find that the numbers are 390 and 399. The median of this set of data is the mean of these two numbers:

$$\boxed{(}\ 390\ \boxed{+}\ 399\ \boxed{)}\ \boxed{\div}\ 2\ \boxed{=}\ 394.5$$

Which fast food types have median numbers of calories below the overall median number of calories?   ***Chicken and roast beef***

Homework Project

15. a. Use your stem-and-leaf plot for the fat content of the fast foods to help you determine the median number of grams of fat in the foods listed.
19.5 grams

b. Do you think the mean number of grams of fat in these fast foods will be greater than or less than the median number? Explain your reasoning. Check your prediction by using a calculator to find the mean.
Sample answer: Greater. There is a high outlier which will raise the mean; 21.9

16. Roller World is ordering new skates. Which would be more useful for the manager to know, the mean, mode, or median skate size of prospective customers? Explain your reasoning. *Sample answer: The mode because that would be the most frequently requested size.*

17. Wanita, a recent high school graduate, is seeking a job in a small tool and die factory. She was told that the average salary is "over $19,000." Upon further inquiry, she obtained the following information.

Type of job	Number employed	Individual salary
President/owner	1	$200,000
Business manager	1	50,000
Supervisor	2	40,000
Foreman	5	24,000
Lathe & drill operator	50	14,000
Secretary	2	12,000
Custodian	1	8,000

a. Is the reported average salary correct? *Yes, to the nearest dollar the average mean is $19,065.*

b. What is the median salary? *$14,000*

c. What is the mode of the salaries? *$14,000*

Share & Summarize

d. Which measure of center represents this salary structure best? Be prepared to explain your reasoning in class.
Sample answer: The mode because 50 of the 62 jobs have a salary of $14,000. By saying the median is $14,000, you would only know that one-half of the employees earn $14,000 or less.

18. For each situation below, choose five whole numbers between 1 and 10 inclusive. Repeats are allowed.

    a. The mean and median of the set are the same.
       Sample answer: 3, 4, 5, 6, 7

    b. The mean of the set is greater than the median of the set.
       Sample answer: 2, 3, 4, 8, 9

    c. The mean of the set is less than the median of the set.
       Sample answer: 2, 6, 7, 8, 9

    d. A mode exists and the mean, median, and mode of the set are the same.
       Sample answer: 2, 5, 5, 5, 8

    e. What is the median of the set with the largest possible mean?
       10, 10, 10, 10, 10; median = 10

19. A histogram of the total calories in the fast foods listed on page 24 is shown below.

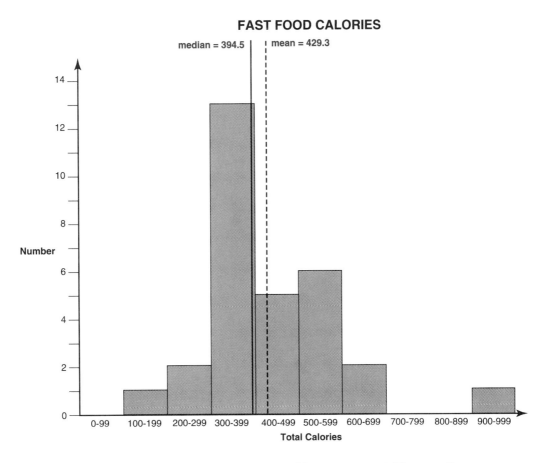

FAST FOOD CALORIES

a. What does the solid vertical line represent? *The median.*

b. What does the dashed vertical line represent? *The mean.*

c. How are these two lines related? Explain this relationship in terms of the general shape of the histogram.
    Sample answer: The mean is greater than the median due to the high outlier.

PARTNER PROJECT

20. Listed below are the top franchises in the U.S. based on a company's age, number of units, start-up costs and growth rates.

FYI
The number of Subway stores more than doubled from 1989 to 1993. In an effort to surpass the 14,000 McDonald's outlets, Subway opens 25 new restaurants a week.

Top Franchises in 1994

Company	Type of business	Minimum Start-up costs
Subway	Submarine Sandwiches	$38,900
McDonald's	Hamburgers	385,000
Burger King Corp.	Hamburgers	73,000
7-Eleven Convenience Stores	Convenience stores	12,500
Mail Boxes Etc.	Postal & Business Services	28,180
Little Caesar's Pizza	Pizza	170,000
Chem-Dry Carpet Drapery & Upholstery Cleaning	Carpet, Upholstery & Drapery Services	3,550
Jani-King	Commercial Cleaning Services	2,500
Snap-On Tools	Retail Hardware	12,600
Coverall North America Inc.	Commercial Cleaning Services	350
Hardee's	Hamburgers	502,200
Re/Max International Inc.	Real Estate Services	60,000
ServiceMaster	Commercial Cleaning Services	7,000
Jazzercise Inc.	Weight-Control/Fitness Centers	1,360
Midas International Corp.	Brakes, Front-End, Mufflers & Shocks	182,000
Dairy Queen	Soft Serve	370,000
Baskin-Robbins USA Co.	Ice Cream, Frozen Yogurt & Shaved Ice	92,000
Choice Hotels International	Hotels & Motels	1,500,000
KFC	Chicken	100,000
Arby's Inc.	Miscellaneous Fast Foods	525,000
Coldwell Banker Residential Affiliates Inc.	Real Estate Services	4,000
GNC Franchising Inc.	Health Food/Vitamin Stores	66,700
Holiday Inn Worldwide	Hotels & Motels	1,150,000
Budget Rent A Car	Auto Rentals	40,000
Dunkin' Donuts	Donuts	175,000

Source: Entrepreneur magazine, January, 1994

a. What type of graph would be most appropriate for representing this set of data? Use a statistical software package to produce the graph. If possible print a copy of the graph. *Histogram; See the Teacher's Answer Key for a sample histogram.*

b. What is the range of this set of data? *$1,499,650*

c. Describe the shape of the graph of this set of data. *See the Teacher's Answer Key.*

d. What kinds of businesses occur most often in this list? What are some possible reasons for their popularity? *Fast foods; Sample answer: low start-up costs, advertising, daily need to eat.*

e. What measure of center would be most appropriate for summarizing this data? Explain the reason(s) for your choice. Use statistical software to compute this statistic. *Sample answer: Median = $66,700; The few very high values will affect the mean.*

f. Locate this measure of center on your graph and draw a vertical line through it. *See students' work.*

g. Compute another measure of center – either the mean or median. Using a different color pen or pencil, locate this on your graph and draw a vertical line through it. *Sample answer: Mean = $220,073.60; See students' work.*

h. How are these two lines related? Explain this relationship in terms of the general shape of the graph of the distribution. *See the Teacher's Answer Key.*

Share & Summarize

i. Write a summary of conclusions you can draw from your graph and the measures of center. Be prepared to share your conclusions with the class. *See the Teacher's Answer Key.*

21. Extension Histograms and grouped frequency tables like the one below are useful for summarizing large sets of data. One drawback is that they do not retain the actual numbers. Thus, measures of center such as the mean and median cannot be computed exactly.

Population (in millions)	1970	1990
Under 5 years old	17.2	18.8
5-19 years old	59.9	53.0
20-24 years old	16.4	19.1
25-34 years old	24.9	43.2
35-44 years old	23.1	37.4
45-64 years old	41.8	40.2
65 years old and over	20.0	31.1

Source: U.S. Bureau of the Census, Statistical Abstract of the United States: 1994

a. Using the information in the table, approximate the mean age of the U.S. population in 1970. Approximate the mean age of the U.S. population in 1990. What can you conclude? *Sample answer: An approximate mean for 1970 is 32 and for 1990 it is 35. (The midpoint for the 65 and over interval was chosen as 75.); The U.S. population is collectively getting older.*

b. Share your method for approximating the mean of a grouped frequency table with your classmates. On the basis of their input, write a procedure (a set of directions) that others could use to approximate means of grouped frequency tables. **See the Teacher's Answer Key.**

c. Approximate the median age of the U.S. population in 1970. Approximate the median age of the U.S. population in 1990. What can you conclude? **Sample answer: The approximate median age in 1970 was 28.3, and in 1990 it was 38; The population is aging.**

Journal

d. Journal Entry Write a procedure that others could use to approximate the medians of grouped frequency tables. **See the Teacher's Answer Key.**

e. Which approximated measure of center is greater for 1970? for 1990? Locate each measure of center on the respective histogram you made for Exercise 6 on page 31. Draw a vertical line through the point representing each measure of center. How are these lines related in each histogram? **See the Teacher's Answer Key.**

f. For each histogram, is the relationship between the mean and median lines consistent with the information conveyed by the shape of the graph? Explain. **See the Teacher's Answer Key.**

22. Extension A histogram of graduation rates for public high schools for the 50 states and the District of Columbia is shown below.

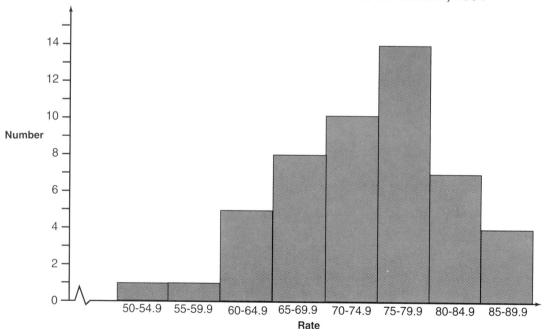

HIGH SCHOOL GRADUATION RATES BY STATE, 1991

a. How many pieces of data was the histogram based on? **51**

b. Using only the graph, estimate the median graduation rate for the U.S. If a vertical line was drawn to represent your estimate, where would it intersect the horizontal axis? **74**

c. Based on the shape of the graph, will the point on the horizontal axis that corresponds with the mean graduation rate be on, to the left of, or to the right of the median line? Explain your reasoning. ***See Teacher's Answer Key.***

d. Verify your conjecture by computing the median and mean. ***Median = 74.5, mean = 74.127***

Journal

23. Journal Entry Based on your experience in this activity, describe a possible relationship between the shape of a histogram and the position of lines that correspond with the median and mean. ***See the Teacher's Answer Key.***

Share & Summarize

24. Journal Entry Write a short paragraph that describes what you think are the main advantages and disadvantages of each of the measures of center – mean, median, mode – for describing a set of data. Be prepared to explain your reasoning to the class. ***See the Teacher's Answer Key.***

Activity 4-2   Patterns in Statistics

Materials

 ruler

 calculator

Suppose the factory whose salary schedule is on page 38 of the previous activity successfully completed a major contract. Each employee, including the president, is awarded an immediate $1,000 increase in salary. What would be the new mean salary for the company?

Before attempting to answer this question, consider the following simpler situations.

The table and **line plot** below show the average monthly temperatures in degrees Fahrenheit (°F) for Kalamazoo, Michigan. The data has been rounded to the nearest degree.

Month	Jan.	Feb.	Mar.	Apr.	May	June	July	Aug.	Sept.	Oct.	Nov.	Dec.
°F	24	27	36	49	60	69	73	72	65	54	40	29

Source: National Climatic Data Center

The mean yearly temperature for Kalamazoo is 49.8°. The mean is located by a small square on the line plot below.

The median yearly temperature is 51.5°. It is identified by a small triangle on the plot.

PARTNER PROJECT

1. a. Suppose, due to global warming, each of the average monthly temperatures increases by 5°. On a separate sheet of paper, draw a number line like the one shown on page 44. Locate the new temperatures on this number line. *See students' work.*

   ● Find the new mean and median yearly temperatures. Locate these on your line plot using a small square and a small triangle as was done for the original data. *Mean = 54.8°, median = 56.5°; See students' work.*
   ● How does the new mean compare with the original mean? *5° larger*
   ● How does the new median compare with the original median? *5° larger*
   ● Describe how your line plot is related to the original line plot. *All points of the second line plot are shifted 5° to the right.*

b. Suppose by the year 2020 average monthly temperatures have each increased 10 degrees over that given in the table. Draw a number line below the one you previously drew. Locate these new temperatures on your second number line. *See students' work.*

   ● Make a conjecture about the new mean yearly temperature for Kalamazoo. Check your conjecture and locate the mean on your second line plot. How does the new mean compare with the original mean? *New mean is 10° more than the original mean. The new mean is 59.8°.*
   ● Make a conjecture about the new median yearly temperature. Check your conjecture and locate the median on the line plot. How does the new median compare with the original median? *The new median is 10° more than the original median. The new median is 61.5°.*
   ● Describe how your second line plot could be obtained from the original line plot. *All points of the first line plot could be shifted 10° to the right to obtain the third line plot.*

c. If the original average monthly temperatures each increase by *n* degrees, what will be the new mean yearly temperature? What will be the new median yearly temperature? *See the Teacher's Answer Key.*

d. Suppose average monthly temperatures as given in the table each decrease by 10 degrees. Draw a number line below the two you've already drawn. Locate these new temperatures on your third number line. *See students' work.*

- Make a conjecture about the new mean yearly temperature for Kalamazoo. Check your conjecture and locate the mean on your third line plot. How does this new mean compare with the original mean? *The new mean is 10° less than the original mean. The new mean is 39.8°.*
- Make a conjecture about the new median yearly temperature. Check your conjecture and locate the median on the line plot. How does this new median compare with the original median? *New median is 10° less than the original median. The new median is 41.5°.*
- Describe how your third line plot could be obtained from the original line plot. *All points of the first line plot could be shifted 10° to the left.*

e. If the original monthly temperatures each decrease by *n* degrees, what will be the new mean yearly temperature? What will be the new median yearly temperature? *See the Teacher's Answer Key.*

2. Suppose the mean of a set of data is represented by $\overline{X}$ (read "*x*-bar").
  a. If a number *c* is added to each piece of data in the set, how could you represent the new mean? $\overline{X} + c$

  b. If a number *c* is subtracted from each piece of data in the set, how could you represent the new mean? $\overline{X} - c$

3. Suppose the median of a distribution is represented by *M*.

  a. If a number *c* is added to each piece of data, how could you represent the new median? *M + c*

  b. If a number *c* is subtracted from each piece of data, how could you represent the new median? *M − c*

4. Answer the question on the new salary distribution posed at the beginning of this activity on page 44. *The new mean salary will be $20,065.*

Share & Summarize

5. Assume a distribution of math test scores has a mode. If the teacher decides to add 5 points to every student's score, how will this affect the mode? Be prepared to explain your reasoning to the class. *The new mode will be 5 points more than the original mode. If all scores are increased by 5, the whole set of data will shift up 5 points, causing the mode to also increase by 5.*

6. A quality control engineer in a factory that manufactures the LT1 engine for Corvettes measures the diameter of each of the eight cylinders of a sample engine at regular intervals. The table and line plot below give the amount of variation (in hundredths of a millimeter) from the design specification for each cylinder of a sampled engine.

Cylinder	1	2	3	4	5	6	7	8
Variation (0.01 mm) from specification	4	9	12	2	8	5	2	7

The mean amount of variation is 6.1 hundredths of a millimeter. It is marked on the graph by a small square.

The median amount of variation is 6 hundredths of a millimeter. It is located on the graph by a small triangle.

FYI
If the diameter of a cylinder is too large, compression wil be lost when fuel is ignited. If the diameter is too small, either the piston won't fit or heat of friction will deform the cylinder.

a. Suppose that a systematic maladjustment in the cylinder boring process doubles the amount of variation in each cylinder. Draw a number line and locate the new amount of variation for each cylinder on it. *See students' work*

● Find the new mean and median variations in cylinder diameters. Locate these on your line plot with a small square and a small triangle as was done for the original data. *New mean = 12.2; new median = 12*

● How does the new mean compare with the original mean? *The new mean is twice the original mean.*

● How does the new median compare with the original median? *The new median is twice the original median.*

● Describe how your line plot is related to the original line plot. *See the Teacher's Answer Key.*

b. Suppose that adjustments to the cylinder boring machine result in reducing the original amount of variation by 50% or a factor of $\frac{1}{2}$ in each cylinder. Draw another number line below the one you previously drew. Locate the new variations in cylinder diameters on your second number line. *See students' work.*

● Make a conjecture about the new mean variation. Check your conjecture and locate the mean on your second line plot. How does the new mean compare with the original mean? *The new mean is half of the original mean. The new mean is 3.05.*

- Make a conjecture about the new median variation. Check your conjecture and locate the median on your second line plot. How does the new median compare with the original median? **_The new median is half of the original median. The new median is 3._**
- Describe how your second line plot is related to the original line plot. **_The line plot is shrunk to half the size of the original plot._**

c. If maladjustments in the cylinder boring process cause the original amount of variation in each cylinder to be multiplied by a number k, what will be the new mean variation in cylinder diameters? What will be the new median variation in cylinder diameters? **_See the Teacher's Answer Key._**

FYI
In some engines, the distance between a cylinder and the piston that moves through it measures between 0.023mm and 0.033mm. That's about one-half the thickness of the average human hair!

7. Suppose the mean of a set of data is represented by $\overline{X}$. If each piece of data in the set is multiplied by a constant c, how could you represent the new mean? $\overline{X} \cdot c$

8. Suppose the median of a set of data is represented by M. If each piece of data in the set is multiplied by a constant c, how could you represent the new median? $M \cdot c$

⬤ HOMEWORK PROJECT

9. Assume the mode score on a 10-item true/false Social Studies test is 6. The teacher records the scores as percents. What is the mode of the percent scores on this quiz? Explain your reasoning. **_See the Teacher's Answer Key._**

10. In general, how does adding a constant to each piece of data in a set of data affect the range of the set? **_The range of the set of data remains the same._**

Share & Summarize

11. In general, how does multiplying each piece of data in a set of data affect the range of the set? Be prepared to defend your answer. **_The range of the set of data is also multiplied by the constant._**

12. **Extension** A formula for converting temperature in degrees Fahrenheit (F) to degrees Celsius (C) is $C = \frac{5}{9} (F - 32)$ or $C = \frac{5}{9} F - \frac{160}{9}$. Look at the temperature data for Kalamazoo at the beginning of this activity on page 44. Without calculating each of the average monthly temperatures in degrees Celsius, determine the mean yearly temperature in degrees Celsius for Kalamazoo. **_9.8°C or approximately 9.9°C_**

13. Extension A set of data consists of five measures represented by X_1, X_2, X_3, X_4, and X_5.

a. Write an expression for the mean, $\overline{X}$, of this set. $\dfrac{X_1 + X_2 + X_3 + X_4 + X_5}{5}$

b. Create a new set of data by adding 10 to each original piece of data.
$X_1 + 10,\ X_2 + 10,\ X_3 + 10,\ X_4 + 10,\ X_5 + 10$

c. Write an expression for the mean of this new set of data.
$\dfrac{X_1 + 10,\ X_2 + 10 + X_3 + 10,\ X_4 + 10,\ X_5 + 10}{5}$

d. Show that the new mean can be represented as $\overline{X} + 10$.

$\dfrac{X_1 + X_2 + X_3 + X_4 + X_5 + 50}{5} = \overline{X} + 10$

e. Show that if a constant number c is added to each data point of the original data, then the new mean is $\overline{X} + c$.   ***See the Teacher's Answer Key.***

f. Can you find the median of the original set of data? Explain.
No. To find the median, you must be able to order the data.

⬤ GROUP PROJECT

14. Refer to the class data table you created in Activity 2-1 on page 17 and placed in your portfolio. Your group is to select one of the variables— height, armspan, thumb circumference, wrist circumference, shoe length, or stride length, and then analyze and report on the data to the class. Share the work in preparing the report.

Your report to the class should include:

a. a histogram of the data and a discussion of the range and overall shape of the graph, including the existence of possible outliers;

b. measures of center and their locations on the histogram;

c. a discussion of which of the measures of center best describes the typical student in your class with respect to your chosen variable;

d. a prediction of the range and measures of center of corresponding data on your class as seniors. Explain the assumptions and reasoning behind your prediction.   ***See students' work.***

Portfolio Assessment

Select an item from this investigation that you feel shows your best work and place it in your portfolio. Explain why you selected it.

More Data Displays

I n the previous investigation, you found that statistics such as the mean and range or the median and range indicate the center and overall spread of a set of data. Neither pair of statistics, however, gave you an indication of how much variation was present in the data. To get a sense of the variation in the data, you had to supplement the statistics by "eyeballing" the data itself, or preferably, by making a graphical display. The shape of the graph indicated the amount of variation.

Computation and use of additional statistics with characteristics similar to the median can aid in describing the amount of variation in a set of data.

Activity 5-1   Box-and-Whisker Plots

Materials

 calculator

 tracing paper

 ruler

 software

 U.S. map

As a first step to describing the amount of variation in total calories of the fast foods listed in Activity 3-2 on page 24, order the data from least to greatest. Recall that since this set has 30 pieces of data, the median is the mean of the middle two (15th and 16th) numbers in this set. You should find that these two numbers are 390 and 399.

$(\quad 390 \quad + \quad 399 \quad) \quad \div \quad 2 \quad = \quad 394.5$

The median of the set of data is 394.5 calories.

 PARTNER PROJECT 1

1. a. Using the ordered set of data you created, find the median of the set of data less than the median. This number is called the **lower quartile**. ***8th number = 340***

b. What fraction or percent of the pieces of data are less than or equal to the lower quartile? Explain your reasoning. ***See the Teacher's Answer Key.***

c. Find the median of the set of data greater than the median. This number is called the **upper quartile**. ***500***

d. What fraction or percent of the pieces of data are less than or equal to the upper quartile? Explain your reasoning. ***Same answer as in Exercise 1b.***

e. What fraction or percent of the pieces of data should fall between the lower and upper quartiles? Explain your reasoning. ***One-half or 50%. If 25% of the data value are above and below the quartiles, then 50% is between the lower and upper quartiles.***

 FYI
In 1994, the Third National Health and Nutrition Examination Survey found that Americans' consumption of fat as a percentage of calories is down to 34%, and our blood-cholesterol levels are down 8% since 1960. But our daily calorie intake is up an average of 231 calories.

Source: Vitality, July, 1994

2. The **five-number summary** of the distribution of total calories in fast foods is shown below. It consists of the least value (LV), the lower quartile (LQ), the median (M), the upper quartile (UQ), and the greatest value (GV).

LV	LQ	M	UQ	GV
198	340	394.5	500	935

What can you conclude from these numbers about the variability of total calories in the fast foods?   *See the Teacher's Answer Key.*

3. Trace the histogram of total calories in fast foods shown below.

   a. Locate the points that correspond with the lower and upper quartiles. Draw vertical lines through each of these points.   *See below.*

   b. Locate the point that corresponds to the median and draw a vertical line through this point.   *See below.*

   c. Locate the points that corresond to the least and greatest values and draw vertical lines through these points.   *See below.*

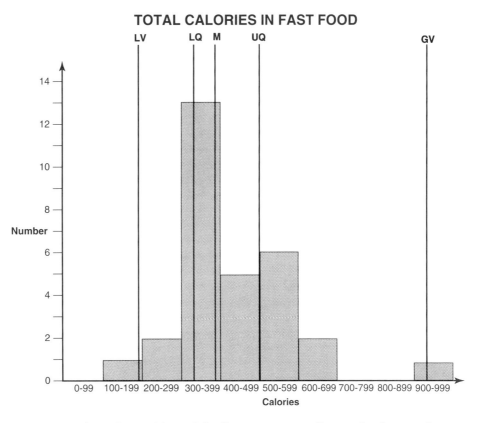

TOTAL CALORIES IN FAST FOOD

   d. How does the position of the lines corresponding to the five-number summary relate to the shape of the graph?   *See the Teacher's Answer Key.*

4. The graph below is a representation of the five-number summary of the data on total calories. It is called a **box-and-whisker plot**. Box-and-whisker plots can be drawn vertically as shown on the left or horizontally as shown on the right. The scale on the number line is based on the range of data. The width of the box can be any convenient size.

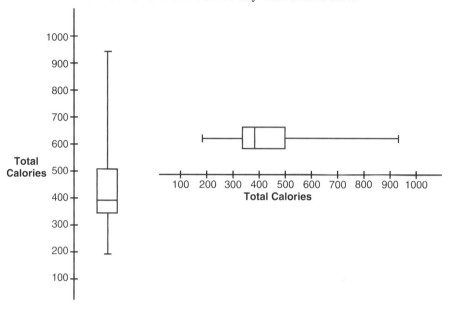

a. What do the ends of the box correspond to? *The upper and lower quartiles*

b. What does the line segment within the box correspond to? *The median*

c. The difference between the upper and lower quartile is called the **interquartile range**. How is the interquartile range represented in the box-and-whisker plot? *The length of the box represents the spread within the middle 50% of the set of data.*

d. Note that the segment representing the median is closer to the lower end of the box. What does this say about the set of data? *See the Teacher's Answer key.*

e. What do the two segments (**whiskers**) extending from the box represent? *The whiskers represent the upper and lower 25% of the data.*

f. Note that the two whiskers are of different lengths. What does this say about the set of data? *See the Teacher's Answer Key.*

g. Looking at a box-and-whisker plot, you can quickly see the center and spread of a set of data. How does a box-and-whisker plot show variation in the data?
Variation can be seen in the length of the box, the position of the median in the box, and the length of the whiskers.

5. The histogram of the total calorie data on page 51 shows a gap because of an outlier, the Burger King Double Whopper with Cheese.

   a. Do the box-and-whisker plots on the previous page suggest to the viewer that there is an outlier in the data? *No*

   b. What is the largest value in the table you created at the beginning of this activity other than 935, which is an outlier? *685*

   c. In statistics, an *outlier* is defined as any value that is at least 1.5 times the interquartile range above the upper quartile or below the lower quartile. In the box-and-whisker plots below, the position of the outlier has been identified by an asterisk. The whisker has been drawn to the greatest value that is not an outlier.

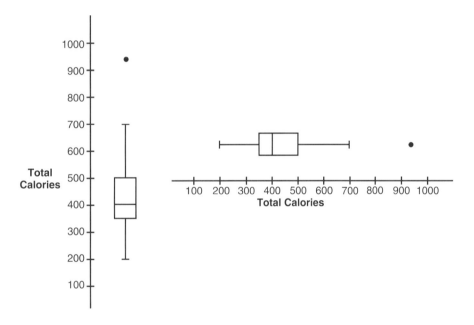

   d. Based on the modified box-and-whisker plot, would you change your answer to Exercise 4 f ? Explain. *Yes. The whiskers are close to the same length, so the spread of the upper 25% and the lower 25% of the set of data are similar.*

6. The table below lists the fast foods ordered in terms of their salt content.

Company	Fast food	Sodium (mg)
Kentucky Fried Chicken	Lite'n Crispy (4 pieces)	354
Burger King	Hamburger Deluxe	496
Wendy's	Single (plain)	500
Kentucky Fried Chicken	Original Recipe (4 pieces)	575
McDonald's	Chicken McNuggets (6)	580
Arby's	Regular Roast Beef	588
Kentucky Fried Chicken	Extra Crispy (4 pieces)	638
McDonald's	Quarter Pounder	650
McDonald's	McLean Deluxe	670
Arby's	French Dip	678
Wendy's	Chicken (regular)	725
Hardee's	Big Deluxe Burger	760
Burger King	BK Broiler Chicken	764
McDonald's	McChicken	770
Wendy's	Fish Fillet Sandwich	780
Arby's	Super Roast Beef	798
Wendy's	Grilled Chicken	815
Burger King	Whopper	865
Burger King	Ocean Catch Fish Filet	879
McDonald's	Big Mac	890
Hardee's	Grilled Chicken	890
McDonald's	Filet-O-Fish	930
Arby's	Fish Fillet	994
Hardee's	Fisherman's Fillet	1030
Arby's	Turkey Deluxe	1047
Hardee's	Chicken Fillet	1060
Wendy's	Big Classic	1085
Burger King	Double Whopper w/Cheese	1245
Hardee's	Turkey Club	1280
Burger King	Chicken Sandwich	1417

a. Compute the five-number summary: least value, lower quartile, median, upper quartile, and greatest value.
LV = 354; LQ = 650; M = 789; UQ = 994; GV = 1,417

b. Does the data have any outliers? *Answers may vary but generally no.*

c. Make a box-and-whisker plot for the salt content of the fast foods. *See the Teacher's Answer Key.*

d. Compare your box-and-whisker plot for salt content with the box-and-whisker plot for total calories. Which box-and-whisker plot is more symmetric? Explain your reasoning.   *See the Teacher's Answer Key.*

7. Extension

a. Based on the shape of the box-and-whisker plot in Exercise 5, where do you think the mean number of calories would be located? Explain the reasoning behind your choice of location.   *See the Teacher's Answer Key.*

b. Check your conjecture by referring to the chart you made in Investigation 4 on page 35.   *mean = 429.3; median = 394.5*

c. Based on the box-and-whisker plot in Exercise 6, do you think the mean and median will be relatively closer together in the case of salt content as compared with total calories? Explain your reasoning. Check your conjecture.   *See the Teacher's Answer Key.*

⬤ PARTNER PROJECT 2

Graphing Calculator Activity

You can learn how to use a graphing calculator to draw box-and-whisker plots in Activity 4 on page 71.

8. Box-and-whisker plots are reasonably easy to draw once a data set has been ordered. However, ordering a set of data can be very time consuming. Statistical software packages can be used to readily produce box-and-whisker plots once the data has been entered.

a. Use software to produce a box-and-whisker plot of the U.S. high school graduation rates shown on page 32.   *See the Teacher's Answer Key.*

b. Compare your box-and-whisker plot with the graph for this data shown on page 42. Which graphical display seems more informative? Explain your reasoning.   *See the Teacher's Answer Key.*

Histograms (or stem-and-leaf plots for small data sets) when accompanied by the median and quartile points, are usually more informative than box-and-whisker plots. However, box-and-whisker plots are more useful when comparing data sets with respect to the same variable.

9. a. Separate the state and District of Columbia graduation rates into two groups:
  ● western states; those west of the Mississippi River, including Louisiana and Minnesota,
  ● eastern states; those east of the Mississippi River.

b. Use software to enter this data in the appropriate way and then produce side-by-side box-and-whisker plots.   *See the Teacher's Answer Key.*

c. Overall, how do graduation rates in the two parts of the country compare? What are some possible explanations for this difference? *See the Teacher's Answer Key.*

d. Using the box-and-whisker plot, estimate the median and lower and upper quartiles for the eastern states.   *median = 73; lower quartile = 66; upper quartile = 78.5*

e. Visually estimate the median and lower and upper quartiles for the western states.   *median = 76.5; lower quartile = 72.5; upper quartile = 83*

f. Visually estimate the interquartile range for the eastern states by looking at the box-and-whisker plot.   *IQR = 12.9*

g. Visually estimate the interquartile range for the western states.   *IQR = 10.6*

h. Is there more variation in graduation rates among the eastern states or the western states? Explain your reasoning.   *See the Teacher's Answer Key*

i. Check your visual estimates of the statistics in parts d-g by using numerical tools available in the software. Be prepared to share your findings with the class.   *See the Teacher's Answer Key.*

Share & Summarize

10. Extension   Separate the eastern states into northeast and southeast categories. Similarly, separate the western states.

a. Use software to produce four side-by-side box-and-whisker plots. *See the Teacher's Answer Key.*

b. Overall, which region has the highest graduation rate? Which region has the lowest graduation rate?   *Northwest; Southwest*

c. Which region has the greatest range of graduation rates? Which region has the least range of graduation rates?   *Southwest; Southeast*

d. Which region has the greatest variation in graduation rates? Which region has the least variation in graduation rates?   *Northwest; Northeast if you ignore the outlier and focus on the box.*

GROUP PROJECT 1

11. Extension   What would be another way to separate the states and the District of Columbia into four regions that might be of interest to policy makers who are monitoring education in this country?
Sample answer: East Coast, West Coast, East Central, West Central, or Time Zones

12. Refer to the table on fast foods you created at the beginning of this activity on page 50.

a. Compare the total calories in burgers with that in chicken fast foods using side-by-side box-and-whisker plots. *See the Teacher's Answer Key.*

b. Write a summary of conclusions you can draw from a visual comparison of the plots. *See the Teacher's Answer Key.*

c. Would it be reasonable to compare the total calories in chicken and fish using box-and-whisker plots? Explain your reasoning. *See the Teacher's Answer Key.*

HOMEWORK PROJECT 2

For Exercises 13 and 14, you will need to refer to the table on How Fast Foods Compare on page 24.

13. a. Compare the amount of cholesterol in burgers with that in chicken using side-by-side box-and-whisker plots. *See the Teacher's Answer Key.*

b. Write a summary of conclusions you can draw from a visual comparison of the plots. *See the Teacher's Answer Key.*

14. a. Compare the amount of salt in burgers with that in chicken using side-by-side box-and-whisker plots. *See the Teacher's Answer Key.*

b. Write a summary of conclusions you can draw. *See the Teacher's Answer Key.*

15. Separate the data on start-up costs of top U.S. franchises given on page 40 into two groups: food industries and service industries.

a. Use side-by-side box-and-whisker plots to compare the two industries in terms of start-up costs. *See the Teacher's Answer Key.*

b. Write a summary of conclusions you can draw from analysis of these two plots. *See the Teacher's Answer Key.*

c. What factors in addition to start-up costs might a person consider when investigating the opening of a franchise? *Sample answers: amount of work necessary; popularity of the industry; amount of profit expected; and the number of similar franchises in the area.*

16. Extension The program below, written in the BASIC language, accepts as input a set of data and produces an ordered list and the median. It therefore provides three of the five numbers necessary to easily draw a box-and-whisker plot.

a. Study the algorithm and then modify the program so that it also computes and prints the lower and upper quartiles. *See the Teacher's Answer Key.*

b. Modify the program further so that it prints in order the five-number summary. *See the Teacher's Answer Key.*

```
10 REM DESCENDING SORT & MEDIAN PROGRAM
15 HOME
20 DIM X(75)
30 PRINT "THIS PROGRAM WILL ACCEPT"
31 PRINT "UP TO 75 NUMBERS"
35 PRINT
40 PRINT "HOW MANY NUMBERS DO YOU"
41 PRINT "WISH TO INPUT?"
50 INPUT N
51 PRINT
60 PRINT "ENTER A NUMBER AFTER EACH ?"
70 FOR I = 1 TO N
80 INPUT X(I)
90 NEXT I
100 FOR L = 1 TO N
110 FOR J = 1 TO N – L
120 IF X(J) > X(J + 1) THEN 160
130 LET T = X(J + 1)
140 LET X(J + 1) = X(J)
150 LET X(J) = T
160 NEXT J
170 NEXT L
175 PRINT
176 PRINT
177 PRINT "DISTRIBUTION OF DATA"
178 PRINT "IN DESCENDING ORDER"
179 PRINT
180 FOR I = 1 TO N
190 PRINT X(I)
200 NEXT I
210 IF N/2 = INT(N/2) THEN 240
220 LET K = (N + 1)/2
230 GOTO 270
240 LET K = N/2
250 LET M = (X(K) + X(K + 1))/2
260 GOTO 280
270 LET M = X(K)
280 PRINT
290 PRINT "THE MEDIAN IS ";M
300 END
```

Activity 5-2   Measures of Variability

Materials

 calculator

 software

In previous activities, you found that the range of a set of data provides a measure of the overall spread of the data. Statistics such as the mean or median provide an indication of the center of the data. As you have discovered, the choice of which statistic to use to summarize the center of a set of data depends on the question to be answered and the nature of the data itself. The existence of outliers or extreme data points can have a marked influence on the mean. The median on the other hand is not as easily influenced by extreme values.

To describe the variability within a set of data, you have relied primarily on visual interpretation of graphical displays such as stem-and-leaf plots, histograms, or, more recently, box-and-whisker plots. The five-number summary statistics which are represented by box-and-whisker plots are informative. In particular, the interquartile range indicates the amount of variation about the median.

⬤ PARTNER PROJECT 1

1. Scores on a make-up test in English and in Social Studies by ninth-graders are shown below.

English Make-up Test	Social Studies Make-up Test
71	58
68	68
76	95
74	73
94	45
73	76
65	100
69	57
76	76

a. Overall, did the students perform better on the English test or on the Social Studies test? Explain your reasoning and choice of statistics. ***See the Teacher's Answer Key.***

b. On which test was there a greater overall spread in performance? Explain. ***Social Studies. The spread for social studies is 55, and the spread for English is 29.***

c. Compute the five-number summary for each set of make-up test scores. On which test was there greater variation in student performance? Explain your reasoning. ***See the Teacher's Answer Key.***

d. Suppose the top score on the English test was not 94, but another score of 76. Would you change your answer to part a? Explain. ***See the Teacher's Answer Key.***

e. Would the change in test score given in part d affect your conclusion in part c? Explain. ***See the Teacher's Answer Key.***

2. Suppose in answering Exercise 1a, you chose to use the mean and computed it to be $\frac{666}{9}$ or 74. How could you compute the new mean in Exercise 1d without reading nine numbers? ***See the Teacher's Answer Key.***

3. Another way of thinking of the amount of variability in a set of data is in terms of variation about the mean. The two tables below show the scores on the two make-up tests together with the computation of each mean ($\overline{X}$).

a. Copy and complete each table

- Find the distance, or **deviation**, between each test score and the mean ($\overline{X}$).

- Find the average, or mean, of the distances.

English Make-up Test		Social Studies Make-up Test	
Score	Distance from $\overline{X}$	Score	Distance from $\overline{X}$
71	3	58	14
68	3	68	4
76	*2*	95	*23*
74	*0*	73	*1*
94	*20*	45	*27*
73	*1*	76	*4*
65	*9*	100	*28*
69	*5*	57	*15*
76	*2*	76	*4*
sum = 666	sum = *48*	sum = 648	sum = *120*

$\overline{X} = \frac{666}{9}$ or 74   ***Mean distance***

from $\overline{X} = \frac{48}{9}$ ***or*** $5\frac{1}{3}$

$\overline{X} = \frac{648}{9}$ or 72   ***Mean distance***

from $\overline{X} = \frac{120}{9}$ ***or*** $13\frac{1}{3}$

b. The average of the distances between each data point and the mean is called the **mean deviation**. Which set of make-up test scores has the greater mean deviation? ***Social Studies***

c. How does your answer for part b compare with your answer to Exercise 1c ? ***It is the same.***

4. The average monthly temperatures (°F) for Kalamazoo, Michigan are shown below. The data has been rounded to the nearest degree.

a. Find the mean deviation in monthly temperatures for Kalamazoo. *(Mean temperature 50°) Mean deviation = $\frac{188}{12}$ or about 16°.*

b. How do you think the average monthly temperatures for San Francisco, California compare with those of Kalamazoo?   *Sample answer: The winter months will be warmer in San Francisco.*

Kalamazoo Average Temperatures

Month	Temperature
Jan.	24°
Feb.	27°
Mar.	36°
Apr.	49°
May	60°
June	69°
July	73°
Aug.	72°
Sept.	65°
Oct.	54°
Nov.	40°
Dec.	29°

Share & Summarize

c. How do you think the mean deviation in monthly temperatures for San Francisco compares with that for Kalamazoo? Be prepared to explain your reasoning to the class.   *See the Teacher's Answer Key.*

5. Extension   Computing the mean deviation of even a moderately-sized data set can be tedious, even with a calculator. An innovative student proposed the following procedure. "First I order the data from largest to smallest. Then I compute the mean, $\overline{X}$. I find the deviation between each score and the mean until I reach a case where the deviation is less than zero. I ignore this last deviation. I simply add the positive differences, double their sum , and divide by the total number of scores. This procedure takes me one-half the time." Is this method correct? If so, explain why it works. If not, give an example of a set of data for which the procedure fails.   *No; The procedure fails because the values below the mean are not necessarily the same distance from the mean as the values above the mean.*

Another way of measuring the amount of variation in a set of data about the mean is illustrated below. The statistic computed is called the **standard deviation**. It is found by first calculating the average of the square of the distances between each data point and the mean. Then find the square root of this number.

Organizing your work in a table format, as shown below, will help you keep track of each part of the procedure.

Social Studies Make-up Test

Score	Distance from $\overline{X}$	(Distance)^2
58	14	196
68	4	16
95	23	529
73	1	1
45	27	729
76	4	16
100	28	784
57	15	225
76	4	16

sum = 648

$\overline{X}$ = 72

sum = 2512

average = $\frac{2512}{9}$ or about 279.1

standard deviation = $\sqrt{279.1}$ or about

6. a. Find the standard deviation of scores on the English make-up test. *7.9*

   b. Which set of make-up scores has the greater standard deviation?
   Social Studies

   c. How does your answer for part b compare with your answer to Exercise 1c ?   *The results are similar. Social Studies has greater variability.*

Graphing Calculator Activity

You can learn how to use a graphing calculator to find the mean and standard deviation in Activity 5 on page 72.

● GROUP PROJECT

Computing the standard deviation of a set of data requires more calculations than computing the mean deviation. It is, however, the most common statistic for describing the variability within a set of data. Fortunately, statistical software packages and graphing calculators will calculate and display the mean and standard deviation for you once the data has been entered. You should use this technology as a tool to help in answering the remaining questions in this activity.

For Exercises 7-9, you will need to refer to the table on *How Fast Foods Compare* on page 24.

7. a. In terms of calories, is there greater variability among burgers or among the chicken fast foods? Explain.   *The standard deviation for calories in burgers is 181.8. The standard deviation for calories in chicken is 122.5. This means there is greater varaibility in burgers.*

b. Would your answer to part a be different if the outlier, Burger King Whopper with Cheese, was ignored? If so, explain how it would be different. *Yes. The S.D. of burgers would be 105. Therefore, chicken would have greater variability.*

8. a. In terms of cholesterol, is there greater variability among burgers or among the chicken fast foods? Explain. *See the Teacher's Answer Key.*

b. Would your answer to part a be different if the outlier in the data for burgers was ignored? If so, explain how it would be different. *See the Teacher's Answer Key.*

9. In terms of sodium, is there greater variability among burgers or among chicken fast foods? Explain. *See the Teacher's Answer Key.*

THE FAR SIDE   By GARY LARSON

"The golden arches! The golden arches got me!"

The table on the following page gives information on automobile models road tested by Motor Trend magazine during the last two years. Automobiles are organized by manufacturers: General Motors, Ford Motor Company, Chrysler Corporation.

General Motors Model	Acceleration 0-60 (s)	Braking 60-0 (ft)	EPA city (mpg)
Buick LeSabre Limited	8.8	131	18
Buick Regal GS	9.0	143	18
Buick Skylark GS	10.3	135	19
Cadillac Allante	6.7	145	15
Cadillac Brougham	9.4	133	14
Cadillac STS	8.4	144	16
Chevrolet Beretta GTZ	7.7	141	22
Chevrolet Camaro Z28	6.5	132	17
Chevrolet Camaro IROC-Z	5.8	132	16
Chevrolet Caprice Classic	10.3	139	17
Chevrolet Corvette LT1	5.7	115	16
Chevrolet Corvette ZR-1	4.4	109	16
Geo Metro LSi Convertible	13.8	150	40
Geo Prizm GSi	10.0	143	25
Geo Storm Hatchback	10.5	124	30

Ford Motor Company Model	Acceleration 0-60 (s)	Braking 60-0 (ft)	EPA city (mpg)
Ford Crown Victoria LX	9.5	140	18
Ford Escort LX-E	9.3	138	26
Ford Mustang GT	7.3	144	17
Ford Probe GT	8.0	124	21
Ford Taurus LX	9.4	127	18
Ford Taurus SHO	6.8	135	18
Ford Tempo GLS	10.2	137	20
Ford Thunderbird SC	7.4	136	17

Chrysler Model	Acceleration 0-60 (s)	Braking 60-0 (ft)	EPA city (mpg)
Chrysler LeBaron	9.6	170	20
Chrysler Imperial	11.0	153	17
Chrysler New Yorker 5th Ave.	9.7	150	18
Dodge Daytona ES Limited	8.9	144	19
Dodge Monaco ES	10.3	148	17
Dodge Spirit ES	11.0	128	20
Dodge Stealth R/T Turbo	6.4	117	24
Eagle Premier ES Limited	10.6	126	17
Eagle Talon TSi AWD	6.8	136	22

Source: Motor Trend, July 1992

HOMEWORK PROJECT 1

10. For General Motors models, would you expect greater variability in acceleration or braking distances? Explain your reasoning. Check your hypothesis by calculating appropriate statistics. *See the Teacher's Answer Key.*

11. For Ford Motor Company models, would you expect greater variability in braking distances or in miles per gallon? Check your hypothesis by calculating the appropriate statistics. *See the Teacher's Answer Key.*

PARTNER PROJECT 2

12. Suppose you are in the marketing department at Chrysler Corporation.

a. Use a statistical software package to prepare an appropriate graphical display of the EPA city mileage data for the company's tested models. If possible, print a copy of the graph. *See the Teacher's Answer Key*

b. Find appropriate summary statistics for spread, center, and variability. Explain the reason for your choice of statistics. *The range is 7, the median is 19, the mean is 19.3, and the S.D. is 2.309.*

Journal

c. Journal Entry Write a short company memo of the conclusions you can draw from parts a and b. *See the Teacher's Answer Key.*

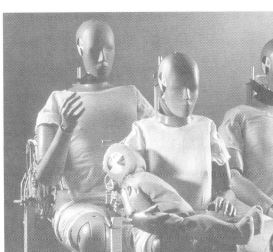

13. Suppose you are a researcher for a consumer products magazine.

a. Use a statistical software package to prepare a graphical comparison of the three company's models with respect to brake effectiveness as measured by braking distance. If possible, print a copy of the graph. *See students' work.*

b. Write a summary of conclusions you can report from analysis of the graph. *See students' work.*

c. Find appropriate statistics that will permit you to compare the three companies in terms of mileage ratings. Explain the reason for your choice of statistics. *See the Teacher's Answer Key.*

14. Suppose adjustments in the emission control system used in each model of General Motors automobiles resulted in a decrease of 1.5 mpg. What would be the effect of this change on the average miles per gallon of all GM cars tested? Explain. *All the average mile per gallon of all GM cars data go down 1.5 units.*

15. Suppose changes in the design of the braking system of Ford automobiles to preserve brake pad life resulted in a new corporate average braking distance for 0-60 mph stops of 140.5 feet. Can you predict the braking distance (0-60) for a Ford Probe GT equipped with the redesigned braking system? Be prepared to explain your reasoning to the class. *See the Teacher's Answer Key.*

16. In Activity 4-2, on pages 44-49, you discovered that transforming the data in a set of data by adding, subtracting, or multiplying by a constant had a predictable effect on the mean, median, and mode. Using the original data of that activity, you will now explore the effects of data transformations on the standard deviation.

a. The table below summarizes the effects on the mean yearly temperature of Kalamazoo, Michigan under transformations applied to each average monthly temperature. Copy and complete this table by finding the standard deviation of the temperature data shown on page 61 and finding the standard deviation of the new data set after applying the transformation rule.

Original mean	Standard deviation yearly temp.	Transformation of monthly temps.	New mean	New standard deviation
49.8	*17.459*	Add 5	*54.8*	*17.459*
49.8	*17.459*	Add 10	*59.8*	*17.459*
49.8	*17.459*	Subtract 10	*39.8*	*17.459*

b. In each case, how does the new standard deviation compare with the original standard deviation? *The new S.D. remains the same as the original S.D.*

c. Suppose in the original set of data, each monthly temperature is increased by n degrees. What will be the standard deviation of the transformed data be? *17.459 degrees*

● HOMEWORK PROJECT 2

17. a. The table below summarizes the effects on the mean variation in cylinder diameters of a sample Corvette engine after different adjustments are made to the cylinder boring machine. Copy and complete the table by finding the standard deviation of the cylinder variation data on page 47 and the standard deviation of the new set of data after applying the transformation rule.

Original mean variation in diameter	Standard deviation of cylinder variations	Transformation	New mean	New standard deviation
6.1	*3.295*	Multiply by 2	12.2	*6.591*
6.1	*3.295*	Multiply by $\frac{1}{2}$	3.05	*1.6475*

b. In each of the cases, how does the new standard deviation compare with the original standard deviation? *When data is doubled, the S.D. is doubled. When data is halved, the S.D. is halved.*

c. Suppose in the original set of data, maladjustments in the cylinder boring process increased the amount of variation in each cylinder by a factor of k. What will the standard deviation of the new data be? *3.295k*

18. Extension Will the standard deviation of a set of data always be greater than the mean deviation? Explain your reasoning. *See the Teacher's Answer Key.*

19. Extension Refer to the data on city gas mileage for the automobiles listed in the table on page 64. Use this data to explore the effects on the shape of a box-and-whisker plot when a set of data set is transformed by:

a. adding a constant to each piece of data *The shape remains the same but it moves left or right.*

b. multiplying each piece of data by a constant *If the constant is greater than 1, the box will stretch and if the constant is less than 1, the box will shrink.*

 Journal

20. Journal Entry Write a summary of your conclusions from Exercise 19 that could be presented to the class.
See students' work.

21. Refer to the class data table you created in Activity 2-1 on page 17 and placed in your portfolio. Separate the data on shoe length into two groups—boys and girls. *For answers to a–d, see students' work.*

a. Compare the shoe lengths of girls and boys using side-by-side box-and-whisker plots.

b. Write a summary of conclusions you can draw from a visual comparison of the two plots.

c. Find the mean and standard deviation for each group. On the basis of your class data and the statistics calculated, do you think a shoe store needs to carry a wider inventory of shoe sizes for girls or boys? Explain.

d. Do you think the medians and interquartile ranges or the means and standard deviations best describe the distributions of shoe lengths? Explain your reasoning.

 **Portfolio Assessment**

Select one of the assignments from this Investigation that you found especially challenging and place it in your portfolio.

Graphing Calculator Activities

Graphing Calculator Activity 1: Plotting Points

The graphics screen of a graphing calculator can represent a coordinate plane. The *x*- and *y*-axes are shown, and each point on the screen is named by an ordered pair. You can plot points on a graphing calculator just as you do on a coordinate grid.

The program below will plot points on the graphics screen. In order to use the program, you must first enter the program into the calculator's memory. To access the program memory, use the following keystrokes.

Enter: PRGM ⇒ 1

Example Plot the points (−5, 3), (7, 1), (3, −4), (−1, −4), and (6, 5) on a graphing calculator.

First, set the range. The notation [−10, 10] by [−8, 8] means a viewing window in which the values along the *x*-axis go from −10 to 10 and the values along the *y*-axis go from −8 to 8.

```
Prgm1: PLOTPTS
:FnOff
:PlotsOff
:ClrDraw
:Lbl 1
:Disp "X="
:Input X
:Disp "Y="
:Input Y
:Pt-On(X, Y)
:Pause
:Disp "PRESS Q TO QUIT,"
:Disp "1 TO PLOT MORE"
:Input A
:If A = 1
:Goto 1
```

Enter: WINDOW ENTER

(−) 10 ENTER 10 ENTER 1 ENTER

(−) 8 ENTER 8 ENTER 1 ENTER

The program is written for use on a TI-82 graphing calculator. If you have a different type of programmable calculator, consult your User's Guide to adapt the program for use on your calculator.

Now run the program.

Enter: PRGM 1 ENTER

Enter the coordinates of each point. They will be graphed as you go. Press ENTER after each point is displayed to continue in the program.

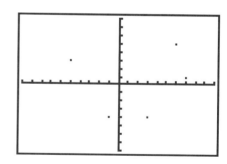

Try This

Use the program to graph each set of points on a graphing calculator. Then sketch the graph. **See students' work.**
1. (9, 1), (−2, 1), (3, 3), (−7, −1)
2. (−12, 1), (15, −5), (−3, −2), (−19, −9)
3. (−0.9, 0.2), (0.5, 1.4), (−2.2, 4.1), (−2.7, −1.3), (0.8, 4.2)
4. (82, 10), (−46, 31), (−29, −57), (84, −66), (72, −47), (99, 19)

Graphing Calculator Activity 2:   Constructing Line Graphs

When you are analyzing a set of data, it is often helpful to look at a graph. One useful graph is a line graph. You can construct a line graph on a graphing calculator.

Example Use a TI-82 graphing calculator to construct a line graph of the data on popcorn sales in the table below.

Unpopped Popcorn Sales in Millions of Pounds

Year	1983	1984	1985	1986	1987	1988	1989	1990	1991	1992
Sales	618	630	670	700	741	807	872	938	1,031.8	1,124.6

First, enter the data into the statistical memory of the calculator. *Be sure to use the ClrList command to clear the lists of information already stored there.*

Enter: STAT   ENTER   *Accesses the statistical lists.*

1983 ENTER 1984 ENTER ... 1992 ENTER   *Stores the years in L1.*

▶ 618 ENTER 630 ENTER ... 1124.6 ENTER   *Stores the pounds in L2.*

Now choose the type of statistical plot you want to display.

Enter: 2nd   STAT PLOT   ENTER   *Accesses the menu for the first statistical graph.*

Use the arrow and ENTER keys to highlight your selections for the graph. Select "On", the line graph, "L1" as the Xlist, "L2" as the Ylist, and "•" for the marks.

Before the calculator can generate the graph, you must enter the range of the *x* and *y* values for the graphics window. A range of [1980, 1995] with a scale of 2 for *x* and [0, 1200] with a scale of 100 for *y* is appropriate for this data.

Enter: WINDOW ENTER 1980 ENTER
1995 ENTER 2 ENTER 0
ENTER 1200 ENTER 100

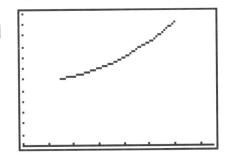

To create the graph, press GRAPH .

● **Try This** *See the Teacher's Answer Key.*

Use a TI-82 graphing calculator to create a line graph of the data.

Percentage of Households with Televisions that have Cable Television

Year	1976	1978	1980	1982	1984	1986	1988	1990	1992
Subscribers	15.1	17.9	22.6	35.0	43.7	48.1	53.8	59.0	61.5

Graphing Calculator Activity 3: Histograms

You can use a graphing calculator to construct statistical graphs as well as graphs of functions. A **histogram** is a statistical graph that displays a set of data as bars of different lengths.

Before you enter a set of data to graph, it is important to clear the statistical memory. If you do not clear the memory, you may store the data in with an old set of data and produce incorrect graphs. To clear List 1 of the statistical memory on a TI-82, press ⎡STAT⎤ 4 ⎡2nd⎤ ⎡L1⎤ .

Example Use a TI-82 graphing calculator to create a histogram of the record high temperatures for each of the states.

112	100	127	120	134	118	105	110	109	112
100	118	117	116	118	121	114	114	105	109
107	112	114	115	118	117	118	122	106	110
116	108	110	121	113	120	119	111	104	111
120	113	120	117	105	110	118	112	114	114

The calculator will use the value you enter for the scale factor on the x-axis to automatically determine the width and number of bars in the histogram.

First, set the range for the graph. Use the range values [100, 135] by [0, 20] with a scale factor of 5 on the x-axis and 2 on the y-axis.

Enter: ⎡WINDOW⎤ ⎡ENTER⎤ 100 ⎡ENTER⎤ 135 ⎡ENTER⎤ 5 ⎡ENTER⎤ 0
⎡ENTER⎤ 20 ⎡ENTER⎤ 2 ⎡ENTER⎤

Now enter the data into the memory and draw the graph.

Enter: ⎡STAT⎤ ⎡ENTER⎤ *Accesses the statistical lists.*

112 ⎡ENTER⎤ 100 ⎡ENTER⎤ 127 ⎡ENTER⎤ ... 114 ⎡ENTER⎤

⎡2nd⎤ ⎡STAT PLOT⎤ ⎡ENTER⎤ *Accesses the menu for the first statistical graph.*

Use the arrow and ⎡ENTER⎤ keys to highlight "On", histogram, "L1" as the Xlist, and "1" as the frequency. Press ⎡GRAPH⎤ to complete the histogram.

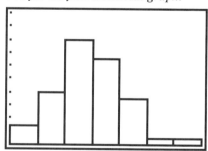

● **Try This** *See the Teacher's Answer Key.*

Use a TI-82 graphing calculator to create a histogram of the ages of the United States presidents at inauguration listed below using intervals of 5. Then make a second histogram using intervals of 3.

57	61	57	57	58	57	61	54	68	51	49
64	50	48	65	52	56	46	54	49	51	47
55	55	54	42	51	56	55	51	54	51	60
62	43	55	56	61	52	69	64	46		

Graphing Calculator Activity 4:   Box-and-Whisker Plots

Box-and-whisker plots summarize a set of data using the median, the upper and lower quartiles, and the extreme values. You can use a TI-82 graphing calculator to create box-and-whisker plots.

Example The table below shows median home prices for several U.S. cities for April 1993. Use a TI-82 graphing calculator to make a box-and-whisker plot for the data.

City	Home Price	City	Home Price	City	Home Price	City	Home Price
Baltimore, MD	$113,200	El Paso, TX	$67,900	Memphis, TN	$84,200	Portland, OR	$99,600
Birmingham, AL	$89,000	Indianapolis, IN	$83,800	Mobile, AL	$66,200	Salt Lake City, UT	$79,000
Boston, MA	$165,200	Kansas City, MO	$79,100	New Orleans, LA	$73,000	Spokane, WA	$79,100
Charleston, SC	$86,200	Los Angeles, CA	$199,700	Omaha, NE	$64,300	Toledo, OH	$65,700
Denver, CO	$96,300	Louisville, KY	$69,900	Philadelphia, PA	$108,900	Washington, D.C.	$153,500

First set the range.

Enter: [WINDOW] [ENTER] 60000 [ENTER] 200000 [ENTER]
10000 [ENTER] [(-)] 3 [ENTER] 7 [ENTER] 1 [ENTER]

Next, clear the statistical memory and enter the data.

Enter: [STAT] 4 [2nd] [L1] [ENTER]
[STAT] [ENTER] 113200 [ENTER]
89000 [ENTER] ... 153500 [ENTER]

Now select the type of graph from the StatPlot menu. Press [2nd] [STAT PLOT] [ENTER] to open the menu and then use the arrow and [ENTER] keys to select "On", the box-and-whisker plot, "L1" as the Xlist, and "1" as the frequency. Press [GRAPH] to view the box-and-whisker plot.

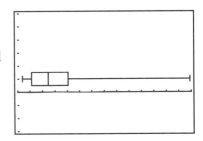

● Try This

Use a TI-82 graphing calculator to create a box-and-whisker plot for each set of data. *See the Teacher's Answer Key.*

1. 21   30   17   19   21   18   27   30   21   21
   30   28   29   21   29   25   28   29   22   27

2. The table below shows the percentage of eligible voters who participated in Elections. *See the Teacher's Answer Key.*

Year	1932	1936	1940	1944	1948	1952	1956	1960	1964	1968	1972	1976	1980	1984	1988	1992
Percentage	52.4	56.0	58.9	56.0	51.1	61.6	59.3	62.8	61.9	60.9	55.2	53.5	54.0	53.1	50.2	55.9

Graphing Calculator Activity 5:   Standard Deviation

In addition to graphing, graphing calculators can be used to perform computations, including finding statistical values for a set of data. One of the values you can find is the standard deviation.

You must clear all of the statistical memories on your calculator before performing any computations. If you forget to clear the memories, your calculations may include old data values causing your results to be incorrect.

Enter: ⎡STAT⎤ 4 ⎡2nd⎤ ⎡L1⎤ ⎡ENTER⎤ *Clears list L1 in statistical memory.*

Example The table below shows the number of millions of people who speak the eighteen most widely used languages as of 1993. Find the mean and the standard deviation of the data.

Language	People	Language	People	Language	People
Arabic	214	Japanese	126	Punjabi	92
Bengali	192	Korean	74	Russian	291
English	463	Malay-Indonesian	152	Spanish	371
French	124	Mandarin	930	Tamil	68
German	120	Marathi	68	Telugu	72
Hindi	400	Portuguese	179	Urdu	98

If you make a mistake entering the data, use the arrow keys to move to the incorrect data and enter the correct value. Use ⎡DEL⎤ to delete an incorrect data value. To insert data at a desired point, press ⎡2nd⎤ ⎡INS⎤ and enter the data.

Enter the data into list L1 in the statistical memory.

Enter: ⎡STAT⎤ ⎡ENTER⎤ *Accesses the statistical lists.*

   214 ⎡ENTER⎤ 192 ⎡ENTER⎤ 463 ⎡ENTER⎤ … 98 ⎡ENTER⎤

After you finish entering the data, press ⎡STAT⎤ ⎡▶⎤ 1 ⎡ENTER⎤ to calculate the statistical values. Notice that the calculator displays many statistics at one time. x denotes the mean, and σx is the standard deviation. To the nearest tenth, the mean number of millions of people speaking these languages is 224.1, and the standard deviation is 208.0.

● Try This

Find the mean and the standard deviation of each set of data. Round your answers to the nearest tenth. $\bar{x} = 30.3$, $\sigma x = 5.6$

1. 46 42 29 29 26 28 31 29 30 35
   33 32 22 21 27 22 28 29 31 26

2. The table below shows the best selling videos as of 1991. **2.** $\bar{x} = 9.2$, $\sigma x = 2.6$

Video	Millions	Video	Millions
E.T. the Extra Terrestrial	15.1	Who Framed Roger Rabbit?	8.5
Batman	11.5	Cinderella	8.5
Bambi	10.5	PeterPan	7.6
The Little Mermaid	9.0	Pretty Woman	6.2
Teenage Mutant Ninja Turtles	8.8	Honey, I Shrunk the Kids	5.8

Glossary

B

Back-to-back stem-and-leaf plot (p. 28) A type of stem-and-leaf plot that is used to compare two used for the leaves of both plots.

Example

December Temperatures		July Temperatures
9	1	
5 3 2	2	
1 1 0	3	
	4	
	5	
	6	5
	7	2 0
9|1 = 19	8	3 5 7
	9	2

9|1 = 19   9|2 = 92

Box-and-whisker plot (p. 52) A graph that uses a number line to display the quartiles and extreme values in a set of data.

Example

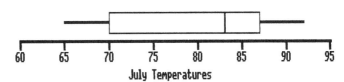

C

Congruent (p. 7) Having the same measure.

Example Two line segments of equal length are congruent.

D

Deviation (p. 60) The difference between a value in a set of data and a fixed number such as the mean of the set of data.

Example If the mean of a set of data is 9, and the set of data contains the value 6, then 6 has a deviation of 3.

Double line graph
(p. 18)

A line graph that displays two sets of data for comparison.

Example

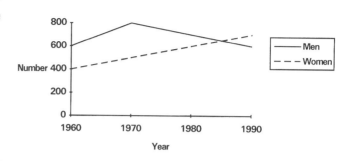

F

Five-number summary
(p. 51)

Five values that represent the least value (LV), lower quartile (LQ), median (M), upper quartile (UQ), and greatest value (GV) of a set of data.

Example

The five-number summary of the scores 67, 72, 76, 85, 94, and 97 is: $LV = 67$, $LQ = 72$, $M = 80.5$, $UQ = 94$, $GV = 97$.

Frequency table (p. 29)

A table that displays how frequently each value in a set of data occurs.

Example

Interval	Tally	Frequency
1-50	|	1
51-100	|||	3
101-150	⦀|	6
151-200	||	2

H

Histogram (p. 29)

A special kind of bar graph that displays the frequency of data that has been organized into equal intervals. The intervals cover all possible values of data. Therefore, there are no spaces between the bars of the histogram.

Example

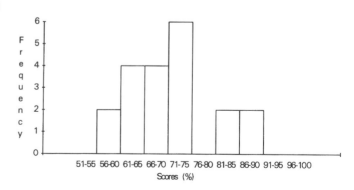

Horizontal axis (p. 21)   The base line of a graph with intervals displayed left to right.

   Example   The line representing "Year" is the horizontal axis.

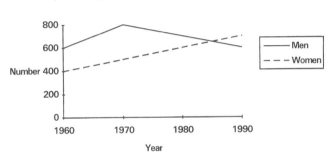

Interquartile range (p. 52)   The difference between the upper quartile and the lower quartile of a set of data.

   Example   If the UQ is 200 and LQ is 75, the interquartile range is 200 − 75 or 125.

L

Line plot (p. 44)   A graph that uses a symbol, such as X, above a number on a number line to indicate each
time a number occurs in a set of data.

   Example

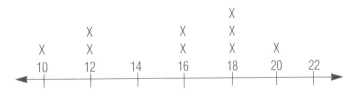

Lower quartile (p. 50)   A value that divides the lower half of a set of data into two equal parts.

   Example   The lower quartile of the set containing 1, 2, 7, 18, 25, 36, 70, 91, 99, and 102 is 7.

M

Mean (p. 36)   The sum of the values in a set of data divided by the number of values in the set.

   Example   The mean of 2, 3, and 7 is $(2 + 3 + 7) \div 3$ or 4.

Mean deviation (p. 60)	The mean of the absolute values of the deviation between each value in a set of data and the mean of all the data.
Example	A set of data that contains 71, 62, and 89 has a mean of 74 and mean deviation of $(3 + 12 + 15) \div 3$ or 10.
Measure of center (p. 34)	An average value that is most representative of an entire set of data.
Example	The most commonly used measures of center are mean, median, and mode.
Median (p. 35)	The middle number in an ordered set of data. If there are two middle numbers, the median is their mean.
Example	The median in a set of data that contains the values 3, 4, 6, 8, and 12 is 6.
Mode (p. 36)	The number that occurs most often in a set of data.
Example	The mode in a set of data that contains 21, 23, 23, and 25 is 23.

O

Outlier (p. 36)	A value in a set of data that is much higher or much lower than the rest of the data.
Example	The outlier in a set of data that contains 2, 3, 5, and 89 is 89.

P

Perimeter (p. 2)	The distance around a geometric figure.
Example	If the length of a side of a square is one unit, the perimeter is 4 units.

R

Range (p. 34)	The difference between the greatest and least values in a set of data.
Example	The range of a set of data that contains 102, 115, 250, and 325 is $325 - 102$ or 223.
Regular polygon (p. 6)	A polygon having all sides congruent and all angles congruent.
Example	Squares and equilateral triangles are regular polygons.

S

Standard deviation
(p. 62)
A measure of the average amount by which individual items of data deviate from the mean of all the data. The standard deviation is the the square root of the mean of the squares of the deviations from the mean.

Example
In a set of data containing 10, 12, 18, and 36, the mean is 19, and the standard deviation is:

$$\sqrt{\frac{(10-19)^2 + (12-19)^2 + (18-19)^2 + (36-19)^2}{4}}$$ or about 10.2.

Stem-and-leaf plot
(p. 25)
A graph where each of the digits in the greatest place values of the data values are the stems and the digits of the next greatest place values are the leaves.

Example

```
           1 | 1 6
           2 | 0
           3 | 4
stems →    4 | 1  3  4  ← leaves
           5 | 7
```

T

Tiling pattern (p. 6)
An arrangement of polygons that covers a flat surface without any overlapping or gaps.

Example

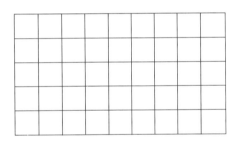

U

Upper quartile (p. 50)
A value that divides the upper half of a set of data into two equal parts.

Example
The upper quartile of 76, 82, 90, 95, 102, and 110 is 102.

V

Variation (p. 25)
A measure of the spread in the values in a set of data.

Example
If there are two sets of values, set A, containing 1, 2, and 7, and set B, containing 1, 3, and 18, then set B has a greater variation since the spread of values (1 to 18) is greater.

Vertical axis (p. 21)   In a graph, the line perpendicular to the horizontal axis, which represents values of data.

Example   The line representing "Number" is the vertical axis.

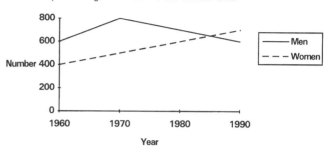

W

Whiskers (p. 52)   The two segments extending from the box in a box-and-whisker plot. They represent the upper and lower 25% of the data.

Example   The whiskers on the box-and-whisker plot below are the segments extending from 10 to 20 and from 55 to 60.

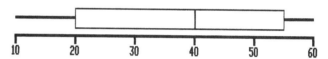

Index

Photo Credits

Cover, (outfielder) Adamsmith Productions/Westlight, (car) Chuck Kuhn/The Image Bank, (thermometer) Aaron Haupt; **v**, KS Studios; **1**, BLT Productions/Brent Turner; **6**, Robert Frerck/Woodfin Camp & Associates; **10**, Todd Yarrington; **12**, Rick Weber; **13**, Tracy I. Borland; **15**, Culver Pictures; **19**, Doug Martin; **25**, Rick Weber; **32**, Ken Frick; **38**, Doug Martin; **40**, KS Studios; **43**, Ken Frick; **44**, file photo; **44-45**, Johnny Johnson; **57**, (**l**) Cathy Cheney/Stock Boston, (**r**) Ewing Galloway; **61**, NASA/Science Source/Photo Researchers Inc.; **63**, THE FAR SIDE cartoon by Gary Larson is reprinted by permission of Chronicle Features, San Francisco, CA. All rights reserved.; **65**, Andy Sacks/Tony Stone Images; **68, 69, 70, 71, 72**, Matt Meadows.

.